natural Accents

Outdoor-Inspired Interior Design & Decor

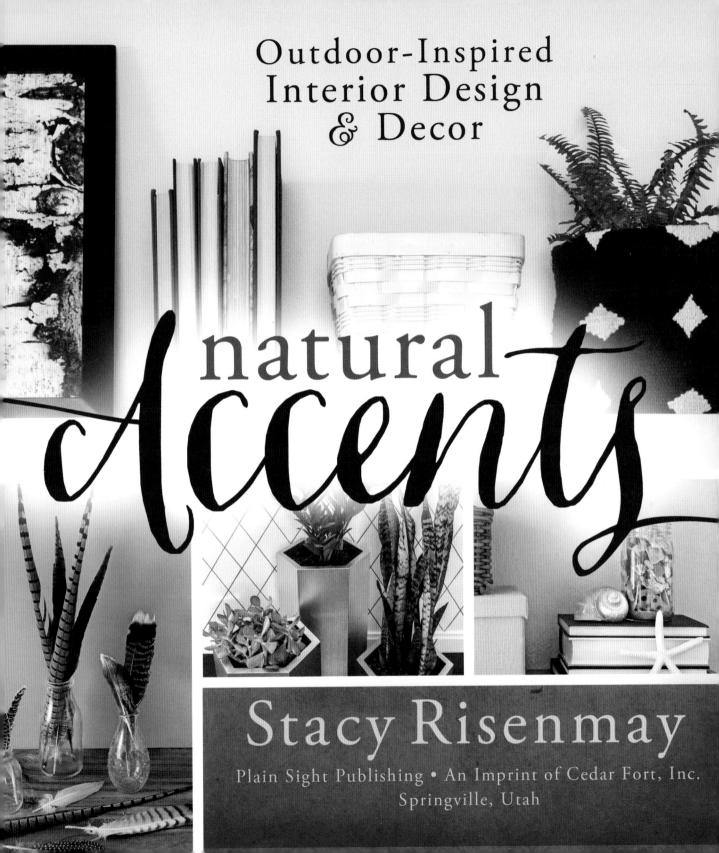

Outdoor-Inspired
Interior Design
& Decor

natural Accents

Stacy Risenmay

Plain Sight Publishing • An Imprint of Cedar Fort, Inc.
Springville, Utah

No part of this book may be reproduced in any form whatsoever, whether by graphic, visual, electronic, film, microfilm, tape recording, or any other means, without prior written permission of the publisher, except in the case of brief passages embodied in critical reviews and articles.

The views expressed within this work are the sole responsibility of the author and do not necessarily reflect the position of Cedar Fort, Inc., or any other entity. Permission for the use of sources, graphics, and photos is also solely the responsibility of the author.

ISBN 13: 978-1-4621-1640-9

Published by Plain Sight Publishing, an imprint of Cedar Fort, Inc.
2373 W. 700 S., Springville, UT 84663
Distributed by Cedar Fort, Inc., www.cedarfort.com

LIBRARY OF CONGRESS CATALOGING-IN-PUBLICATION DATA
Risenmay, Stacy, 1979- author.
 Natural accents / Stacy Risenmay.
    pages cm
 Do it yourself projects out of everything natural from rocks and pebbles to sea glass and log stumps.
 Includes bibliographical references and index.
 ISBN 978-1-4621-1640-9 (alk. paper)
 1. Handicraft. 2. Interior decoration. I. Title.

TT857.R57 2015
745.58'4--dc23

2015002279

Cover design by Rebecca J. Greenwood and Lauren Error
Page design by Lauren Error
Cover design © 2015 by Lyle Mortimer
Edited by Eileen Leavitt
Photography by Stacy Risenmay

Printed in the United States of America

10 9 8 7 6 5 4 3 2 1

Printed on acid-free paper

to my parents

To my dad for teaching me to love and respect nature. And for allowing me to roam barefoot through the fields and collect treasures. I miss you.

To my mom for allowing me to create anything and everything despite the mess, for being a creative spirit herself, and for letting me bring all my "treasures" inside.

contents

acknowledgments

I want to thank my Heavenly Father for creating this amazing earth we live on. I see Him in every leaf, shell, and flower. I want to thank Him for answering my prayers and for guiding me on when the right time was to write this book. I could go on and on because, really, I owe everything to Him.

I want shout from the rooftops a giant thank you to my (very patient) husband. I turned our tiny house into a photo studio, a woodworking shop, a florist shop, a garden nursery, and an all-around mess . . . for four months. He not only didn't complain when he came home and had to climb over a sofa in the kitchen to get in only to then have to climb back over so he could pick up pizza (again) for dinner, but he also pitched in and helped wherever he could. He also didn't completely lose it when his perfectionist of a wife told him to re-cut a piece of wood for the third time. Maybe he wanted to, but he didn't. He was so supportive throughout this process. My mom used to say if you could hang wallpaper with your spouse and survive, you could survive anything. Well, this book was our "wallpaper." And we did it, hon! Now let's go take a nap.

My kids are amazing. They are used to having my undivided attention most of the time, and they were very understanding of the time I had to take to get this done. They were my cheerleaders and helped out around the house more than usual, which is a lot. They cheered instead of grumbling when they had yet another picnic in some random place in the house while all the other surfaces were covered in projects. I love them so much. They are my best projects ever.

Blogging has helped me in so many ways. I came out of a shell I didn't know I was in, I gained confidence, and I became more efficient with my time. I also made some friends who have changed my life. They came into my life at a time when I needed it most and have taught me so much. So thank you, my DIY Divas! You amaze me with your talent and your kindness.

Blogging has also brought me friendships with the people that read my blog. I wouldn't be here, writing a book, without you. Thank you for reading, commenting, emailing, and encouraging me along the way. My life is changed for the better because of each one of you. Never any judgment, just support.

I want to take a moment and thank all those who have helped make this book possible by donating items for me to use in the various shoots.

Krista Blair, Nate Berkus, and Target for sending me the things I coveted from Nate's collection. I love every single thing. They have all found permanent places in my home now that the book shoots are over.

My IKEA is better than your IKEA because you don't have a Celeste. I have worked with Celeste at the Draper store in the past through blogging, and when I needed some furniture but had far exceeded my tiny budget, she donated some for me to use.

Olson's Garden Shoppe in Payson, Utah, is where I got a ton of the plants in this book. When I had filled my house to the rafters with plants, they even offered to let me borrow plants for shoots so I didn't have to keep buying them. They have the best houseplant section. I want to put a chair right in the middle of it and just read.

Forget Me Not Flowers and Gifts worked so hard to get me springtime flowers in the middle of December. This was not the most ideal time to be writing this type of book, I found. But they got me all the flowers I needed!

I am thankful for the friends and neighbors who responded when I put out the many Facebook posts asking for random objects like buckets and umbrellas. I guess it is my version of asking for a cup of sugar. Thanks for loaning me the props, guys! I love you all.

And a final thank you to all of you who are reading this. Thank you. Thank you for buying this book and for taking the time to read it.

introduction

I was a tomboy growing up. I spent more time outdoors than in. It was not uncommon to find me barefoot, in overalls, and gathering "treasures" such as rocks, bugs, and feathers. I was lucky enough to grow up in the country, and I took full advantage of all the space by going exploring every chance I got.

When I wasn't outside getting dirty and adding to my many collections, I was inside creating. My mom could never find her glue, tape, or scissors because I had hauled them off somewhere. I try to remember that when my own children disappear with my supplies. I used to sneak into my dad's shed and borrow handsaws, nails, and hammers. I would sit in the woodpile, saw the scrap wood, and then nail it together. As I got older, the handsaw was replaced with power tools.

Another love of mine growing up was telling stories. I would lie in bed at night and tell my parents all sorts of tales, and when I became sleepy, I would say, "to be continued . . . ," and fall asleep. I am not sure if the story ever really ended or if it was just one long adventure. I would also sit down at my mother's typewriter and plunk away. I wrote so many books growing up! I loved the sound of the keys on the typewriter, the smell of the Wite-Out, and the feeling of accomplishment when I pulled out a completed sheet. I didn't stop at just typing out the story. I used cardboard and pretty paper to create a book cover. I illustrated it and stapled it all together, making a pretty legit book for an elementary-aged kid.

This book is a combination of those three passions: my love of creating and of do-it-yourself projects, my love of writing, and my love of nature. I have poured myself into this book, and I hope it inspires you to add a little bit of nature into your home.

A QUICK NOTE ABOUT SAFETY

Anyone can use power tools. Even if you have never used a power tool before, you can learn! It is empowering and addicting once you try. I think the first hurdle to getting started with tools is getting over that initial fear of them. Once you have some hands-on training and use the tools a few times, you will gain the confidence to do even more.

Here are some things to keep in mind:

- Use common sense. For example, don't use power tools in the rain, while on prescription drugs, or around small children.
- Inspect the tool before use.
- Know the tool well enough that you can tell if there is a missing part or if there is something loose or cracked.
- Keep your work space clean.
- Don't wear loose clothing or jewelry that could get in the way or caught in the machine.
- Use the appropriate safety gear.
- Don't get *too* comfortable with the tool. A little fear is healthy. If you are too comfortable with it, you won't respect its power, and you become complacent. That is when you don't pay attention, and you *will* get hurt.
- Remember, it is up you to make sure you are being safe.

You can read the manual and watch or read tutorials online, but working one-on-one or in a small group with someone who knows the tool is really the best way to learn. Find someone who you know that can give you a hands-on lesson about the tools. If you don't have a neighbor, relative, or friend who can help, you can go to home improvement stores (like Home Depot) and attend workshops. Or you can contact your local community college to see if they have classes. However you do it, educate yourself about the tool before trying it out yourself.

gloves

If you are using a heat gun or handling anything sharp, you will want to wear thick leather gloves. To protect your hands from paint and stain, you can wear rubber or latex gloves.

safety glasses

Always use safety goggles or glasses when cutting wood. I also wear them if I am sanding outside and it is windy.

ear plugs

Some tools can be quite loud. Use ear protection of some kind.

mask

If you are staining, sealing, or spray-painting, it might be a good idea to use a mask.

i thank you God for this most amazing day: for the leaping greenly spirits of trees and a blue true dream of sky; and for everything which is natural which is infinite which is yes.[1]

–e. e. cummings

chapter 1: why?

I would like to start by answering the question, why should you add natural elements to your home? I personally love to add touches of nature to my home because of my deep appreciation for the great outdoors. And if you can't be outside, then why not bring some of the outdoor in? But even if you don't share my love of all things nature, there are many other reasons.

Natural elements add texture and depth to your space in a way that nothing else can. Adding texture is something that is often overlooked when designing a space. It affects how a space feels as well as how it looks. Texture is the difference between a space you want to touch and experience and a space that you don't give a second thought to. Whether it is a basket woven from grapevine, a tree stump for a side table, a lush green plant, or some coral on a shelf, adding natural elements is a great way to add visual interest.

Things from nature, especially plants and flowers, breathe life into a space! I could go on and on about the benefits of having plants and flowers in your home. I strongly believe that being surrounded by them—not only in your home but also in your workspace—will lift your spirit, purify the air, bring stress levels down, and add beauty. When I have a vase of flowers on my kitchen table, it suddenly doesn't matter that there are dishes in the sink and crushed Cheerios on the floor. And during our long hard winters, the house-plant on the side table makes me hopeful that spring will come. Being out among God's creations can be very healing and soothing, so it makes sense that having some of those things in our homes would have the same effect.

Decorating with natural elements will also save you money. (Maybe I should have started with this one. I probably would have sold most of you on this concept with that point alone!) Why buy expensive art when you can print an enlargement of a photo you took of a waterfall while on vacation and frame it? Why purchase a centerpiece when you can easily make one using items you gathered in your own backyard? I find that the more I use things from nature, the less I have to purchase and the more creative I get to be in my decorating.

Natural elements make great souvenirs. Whenever we go somewhere as a family, we collect things to bring home to remind us of the fun times we had (because we certainly don't want to remember the screaming in the van on the way there). I guess I never really lost that childhood need to collect things while outside. Whether it is a shell from the beach or a rock from the canyon trail, my family usually comes home with something. We tuck it on a shelf, add it to a jar, or display it in a frame. That kind of souvenir is so much better than a tacky keychain anyway.

I have also found that using things from nature is a great way to involve your husband and children in your decorating. This is something else I feel strongly about. Your home is also their home. They should get to help decorate too! Obviously, I don't give my kids free rein or else we would have full-on Lego and Hot Wheels decor throughout the house.

But if you allow them to display things they have collected, they will feel connected to the space and have a sense of ownership. It makes them feel special. And isn't a home a place where a child should feel special?

Why decorate with things from nature? Because it is easy. Not sure what to do with acorns, pine cones, rocks, and shells? When all else fails, put them in a bowl. Let the simple beauty of the natural element be enough. Within the pages of this book, I'll share several simple DIY projects. I'll also share some simple ways you can style your home using things just as they are. Put it in a bowl, stick it on a shelf, or display it in a vase. It doesn't get much simpler than that!

Here's a quick rundown on the "whys" of decorating with nature:

- Plants and flowers have health benefits
- It saves you money
- It helps you remember places you have been
- It is easy
- Family can help
- And because nature is amazing!

Have I convinced you yet? If not, then maybe the projects and ideas I share in this book will. I hope that you will not only re-create some of these projects but also use them as inspiration to come up with ideas of your own. And I hope you will start to see decorating in a whole new light.

I n all things of
nature there is
something of
the marvelous.[1]

–Aristotle

chapter 2: plants

B efore we jump into decorating with houseplants, I want to talk about how to care for them. If you do not feel confident in keeping them alive, you won't use them in your decorating, no matter how amazing the ideas are.

TAKING CARE OF YOUR HOUSEPLANTS

I am one of those people who believes that everyone should have houseplants. I go one step further and think there should be at least one plant in every room of your house and one on your desk at work. I subscribe to the theory that plants and flowers boost your health and overall well-being. "But what if I've killed every plant I've ever had?" you ask. "What if I've even managed to kill a cactus?" Well, my friends, choosing the right houseplant for you is like dating. You might go through a lot of bad dates, but you will eventually find your match. And hopefully you will have learned something along the way (in both scenarios).

Do Your Research

Like anything else that you want to be successful with, you need to do your homework. While you might luck out, and the plant that you randomly bought while shopping might thrive for a long time, most of us need to know a few key details to get the same results. The most common problem I think people have with houseplants is they either ignore them or over-love them. We have all been guilty of this, myself included.

We see a beautiful plant at the store and make an impulse buy. We weren't even there for a plant! We bring it home, throw away the tag that was stuck in the dirt, plant it in a cute pot, set it somewhere, and hope for the best.

The first mistake in that scenario was that we bought it on impulse, simply based on how it looked. The second mistake was throwing away the tag. The third was not caring enough about it to learn how to keep it alive. If I had a dollar for every houseplant I killed as a newlywed, I could have bought my own garden nursery. It was ridiculous.

To have success, you need to know which plants will do best in your specific space, which plants are easy to care for, and which ones are high-mainte-nance varieties you should steer clear of. Some plants require direct light and lots of it. Some prefer filtered light (like light through a curtain) and some are happy with very little light. Some plants need to be kept moist, while others like drier soil.

Let's address the first mistake we made. We bought the plant because it was pretty, but we didn't know a thing about it. There are some plants that are considered hard to kill. These easy-to-care-for plants are usually pretty common, and you should be able to find most of them at your local nursery or home improvement store. My personal favorites are fid-dleleaf fig tree, snake plant (also known as mother-in-law's tongue), ZZ plant, philodendron, pothos, kalanchoe, and all the different types of succulents. Some others are jade plant, spider plant, cast-iron plant, umbrella tree, prayer plant, aloe, ox tongue, rubber plant, and ponytail palm.

Now for the second mistake: throwing the tag away. The tag is golden! It will, at the very least, tell you the name of the plant. You need to know that so if the tag gets lost, you can look it up online. But most tags (or labels on the pot) will tell you how much water and light the plant needs and how fast it will grow so you know when you should repot it. Some tags will give even more detailed information. If I am buying a certain type of plant for the first time, I keep the tag in my filing cabinet so I can ref-erence it later if needed. But you can at least keep a record somewhere of the name of the plant and look it up if you don't want to hang onto the tag.

The third mistake is not caring enough about the plant to learn how to keep it alive. Referencing the tag is a good start. But I think you should read up on it a little more. For example, what are common problems people have with that type of plant? What should you do if something does happen to it? It always helps to be prepared!

Once you have an idea of what you are looking for, head to the nursery. Make sure you buy a plant that is healthy looking. No need to start off on the wrong foot. The leaves should not be droopy or browning on the edges.

What to Do When Things Go Wrong

Fast-forward to when you have had your plant for a while. Things were going well at first, but now it doesn't look too happy. There could be several things wrong, but there are two main reasons a houseplant may struggle. It goes back to the whole "ignoring" or "over-loving" principles I mentioned earlier.

When I had been married a few years (and was still a card-carrying member of the houseplant mur-derer club), I visited an older gentleman who had a living room full of gorgeous (obviously thriving) houseplants. I asked him what his secret was. He said that he only watered them once a week and didn't give them very much water when he did. Some he watered even less. Less? Good grief. My poor plants ate almost as much as I did. I had been watering mine every time the soil looked dry. And it was dry . . . on the surface. For most plants, the soil needs to dry out or the roots will rot. Maybe you could pick a day of the week as your watering day. Poke your finger into the soil and see if it has dried out. If it is still damp, you can skip the watering.

The other issue is ignoring or forgetting about the plant. Shortly after I started writing my blog, *Not Just a Housewife*, it blossomed into something I had never anticipated. I became busier than I had ever been before. Plus, I had just had my fourth child, which totally threw my schedule into chaos. I starting dropping balls, and one of those balls was checking my plants. I had some casualties. If you are the forgetful type, or if you have a change in your routine, put a reminder with an alarm on your device. Write it on your calendar. Tell a friend to remind you. Something!

Another thing that can go wrong with your plant is that it can go into climate shock. It has likely lived its whole life in a warm, humid greenhouse. Then you bring it home to a completely different climate. I bought a plant a few months ago, and within a week, it started dropping leaves. A week later, it only had five leaves left. I looked up what type of fertilizer was best for this particular plant and ordered some right away. I gave it some and kept to my regular watering schedule, even though my inner plant killer of times past wanted me to water it more. After a month, it started growing new leaves! Today, it has half of its leaves back, so the moral of that story is that if your plant goes into shock, don't give up! It may be that a new houseplant will be overwhelmed by its new environment and will "bite the dust" no matter what you do, but chances are good that it will adapt if it is cared for.

One other thing to note is that plants that are in distress are more susceptible to pests like spider mites. If you can keep your plant properly watered and cared for, the risk of pest attacks diminishes.

Cleaning Your Plant

Yep. I said cleaning. Just like everything else in your house, plants will get dusty. And a dusty plant has problems with photosynthesis, which can make it unhealthy and stressed. Never fear. Dusting houseplants is easy If the leaves are shiny, you can simply wipe them with a damp cloth or sponge. If I can carry a plant to the sink, sometimes I just give it a quick rinse under the tap. Always use lukewarm water. If the leaves are fuzzy, use a clean duster or small paint brush to remove the dust.

Special Care in the Winter

When we heat our homes in the winter, we also dry out the air. This can be a game-changer for a houseplant. Plants give off humidity naturally, so sometimes it can help to group them together. The winter also means shorter days and less light. You may need to move your plant to a sunnier spot. Most plants go dormant in the winter, so they need less watering. They also do not need fertilizer. In some cases, fertilizing a plant while it is dormant can damage it.

HOW TO DECORATE WITH PLANTS

Unique Planters

You are not just limited to pots when it comes to creating a home for your houseplant. You can get creative. You just have to remember a couple of things: drainage and drainage. No, that's not a typo. I meant to put it twice. You should know after reading about caring for plants that those roots will rot if they are not given a chance to dry out a little between waterings. There are always exceptions of course, but that is a general rule.

I have seen antique tins, an old guitar, and filing cabinets all turned into planters. One of my favorite planters is a basket. Most of the time, I set the potted plant right into the basket, but I have also lined baskets with plastic (making sure there is a hole in the bottom) so the dirt doesn't fall out of the gaps in the sides. I used thumbtacks to adhere the plastic to the basket along the inside edge.

Buckets are another easy idea, and they are easy to find. I think the older and more dented, the better, but a new shiny one would look good too. I usually pot plants directly into the bucket after I have used a big nail and hammer to punch some holes in the bottom to allow for drainage.

Glass containers are also a favorite go-to planter. These unique containers add lots of character, and you can use things like mason jars, antique milk bottles, or even decorative glass containers from the craft store. You can drill a drainage hole through the glass (a tutorial will be shared later in this chapter), or you can add gravel to the bottom of the glass container to create a space for excess water to drain into.

You can even create small terrarium of sorts. It is easy, and I will show you how.

supply list:

- glass containers
- spoon
- pea-sized gravel
- activated carbon
- peat moss
- potting soil
- small plants
- spray bottle

small terrariums

Anyone can have a regular plant in a regular pot next to their desk. But what about having a small terrarium filled with fairy-sized ferns? A terrarium is easy to make, and you can use almost any clear glass container. Here I have used a glass pitcher, a round vase, and a tall vase. You could also use jars or canisters. I bought my plants online. I just searched for "small plants for terrariums" and found several sites that sold small plants suitable for a terrarium. Check out my source list in the back of the book for more details about where I bought the plants.

1. CLEAN out your containers. Rinse them well, and let them dry.

2. FILL the bottom of each one with pea-sized gravel. Depending on the type of gravel and how it was packed, you may need to rinse the gravel before adding it. Mine had a lot of dust and sandy residue. Since the terrarium doesn't have a drainage hole, the gravel will act as drainage for the water, keeping it away from the soil and preventing root rot.

3. ADD some activated carbon or charcoal on top of the gravel. You can find it at the pet store (or the pet section of a store) near the fish tank supplies. Activated carbon is what is inside the fish tank filters, and it keeps yucky things from growing in your tank, or in this case, planter.

4. PUT down a layer of peat moss. It acts as a barrier between the gravel and the soil. It is all about protecting those roots!

5. POUR in the soil. I use a potting mix that is for succulents and cactus because it drains well. Make sure what you use is a quality mix and not too dense. Then you can add your plants! I used a spoon to help me get in where my hands didn't fit well.

I don't water my terrariums in the same way I water my other houseplants. I mist them with a sprayer. Keep a small spray bottle in a desk drawer or somewhere else handy so you can spray it when it looks like it might be drying out a bit. They like to stay moist but not overly wet.

Have fun and get creative! Maybe add some polished stones, sticks, or moss to the planter as well. Your coworkers will be jealous of your unique plant, and it will keep you happy while you work.

Maybe you love terrariums as much as I do and you want one a little bigger. . . .

supply list:

- 7 sheets of Plexiglas that are 18 × 24 inches and ¼-inch thick
- Plexiglas knife
- sanding block
- 220-grit sandpaper
- 400-grit sandpaper
- Weld-On #4 and applicator bottle with needle
- carpenter's square

- electrical tape
- base table saw
- ⅛-inch plywood
- ¾-inch MDF or plywood
- nail gun and nails
- wood putty
- stain
- hairpin legs or your choice of legs
- polyurethane
- heat gun (optional)

terrarium side table

I made my first terrarium in the fifth grade out of a soda pop two-liter bottle, and I have been fascinated with them ever since. I needed a side table next to my sofa, and remembering how much fun I had with my terrarium, I decided to create a one-of-a-kind terrarium side table. I made mine from scratch, but you could always use a fish tank or some other existing Plexiglas or glass container. I had specific dimensions for the size of table I wanted, so I tried my hand at welding ("gluing") Plexiglas.

If you want to use an existing Plexiglas container you can skip the next few steps. If you do want to make it from scratch, I suggest practicing the welding process on the scrap pieces you cut off before jumping right into welding the terrarium.

I bought Plexiglas panels at Home Depot. I knew I would never be able to get my cuts as perfect as a factory cut, so I wanted to limit the number of cuts I had to make. I bought 18 × 24-inch panels, and I retain the eighteen-inch width but cut some Plexiglas off the top to make the terrarium shorter. Plexiglas will typically have a protective film over each side. Don't take it off even if it gets in the way while you are working. It will ensure your plastic stays scratch free during this whole process.

all along the way, CHEER and BLESS and BRIGHTEN every passing day

I made my terrarium nineteen inches high. (I also planned on making a base out of wood that would add more height.) My cut edges formed the top of the terrarium. Because they would not have anything glued to them and would have a lid resting on top, imperfection was okay. When you weld Plexiglas, the edges need to be near perfect to bond correctly.

I cut the bottom to 18 × 18⁵/₁₆ inches. (Note: the base is not going to be exactly square if you construct your box the way I did, because the two side panels will rest inside of the front and back panels as you connect them together)

1. CUT your panels using a Plexiglas knife. Most

hardware stores carry it in the section where you find acrylic glass. They are inexpensive and will cut Plexiglas up to ¼-inch thick. Just mark where you need to cut, and using a straight-edge, score the Plexiglas with the knife, drawing the knife over and over the same cut multiple times until you have scored halfway through the Plexiglas sheet. Brace the scored line along the straight edge of your workspace (a table, for example), and snap off the excess.

2. EVEN though the edges that will be welded

together are factory cut, they still have a texture created by the saw blade. You will need to sand them smooth using a sanding block. I started with a 220-grit and finished it with 400-grit. It is important to use the sanding block so the edges don't get rounded at all. Remember, the edges won't bond correctly if they are rounded. Also, you will need to sand from one end to the other each time to ensure that it gets sanded evenly.

You can peel the protective paper away from the edges slightly if it gets in your way as you are sanding. Don't remove it all yet!

3. ONCE all your pieces are cut and sanded, it is

time to start assembling them. (*Now* you can peel off the protective film.)

The thing that bonds the Plexiglas together is not a glue but rather a solvent that "melts" the Plexiglas. It is called Weld-On #4. You will need an applicator bottle with a needle as well. This product is available online. Purchase the bottle and the needle together. You'll also need electrical tape—no substitutes. Other tapes will leave a residue on your Plexiglas and lack the flexibility you'll need to pull the welded table pieces together tightly and hold them securely. I used a carpenter's square to make sure each panel was 100 percent square and level before applying the solvent.

Lay the bottom piece for the terrarium on the table. Adhere tape to the underside, leaving half of the tape lapping over the edge so that it will fold up and help secure the side panels.

4. START with the front panel. Then add the

sides and then the back piece. If, for some reason, your measurements were slightly off, any lip you may have will be on the backside and be less visible. The panels will sit on top of the bottom piece. Once you have the front panel in place, tape it and check that it is square.

5. DON'T fill your applicator bottle all the way

full. I filled mine about halfway or a little less. The solvent is the consistency of water, so if you turn the bottle upside down, it will drip out. Instead, squeeze the upright bottle first, and then flip it over. Nothing will come out until you squeeze again. You will gently squeeze the bottle as you run it along the seam where the two pieces meet on the inside. The capillary action will suck the solvent into the seam. Be careful not to squeeze too much because if the solvent gets on the Plexiglas anywhere other than in the seam, it will leave a mark. If it does drip, leave

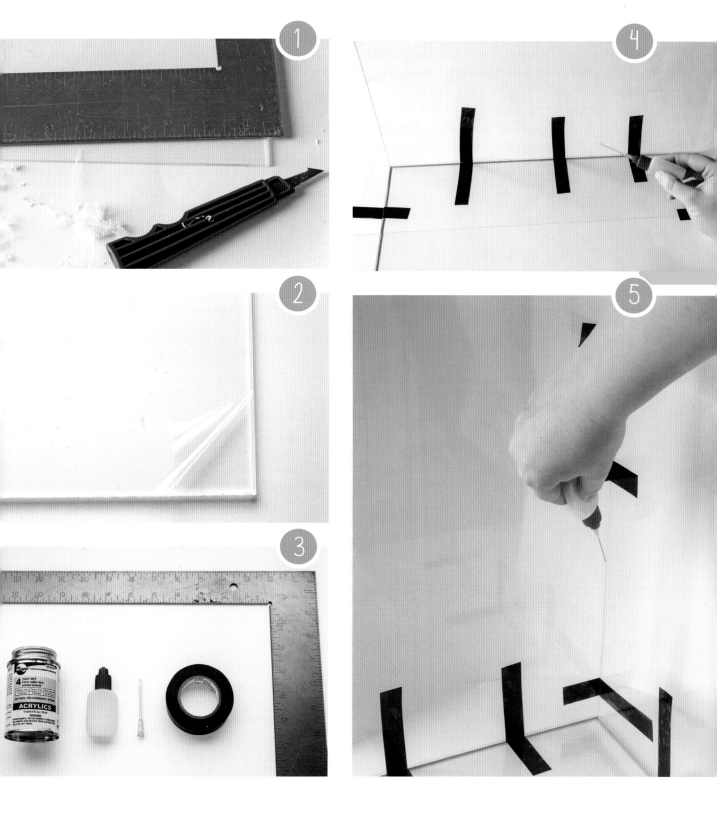

it alone until it dries. If you try to wipe it off, it will just make the mark larger. It is best to practice on scrap pieces first.

6. AFTER the front panel is added and you have waited at least ten minutes, you can add a side panel. Add the solvent along the bottom seam of the side panel, and then add it to the side seam. For the side seam, start about six inches from the bottom corner and go up. The solvent will run down and fill in the empty part of the seam. (In my first attempt, I used solvent on the entire seam, and gravity pulled the liquid down so it puddled at the bottom. Starting six inches above the bottom on the next seam fixed the problem.) Continue to wait ten minutes in between adding each panel. Repeat until all sides are attached.

7. ONCE you have all five panels welded together, it is time to make the top of your terrarium. I didn't want to just place a piece of Plexiglas on top, because I knew it would slide off when bumped, so my simple solution was to cut one piece of Plexiglas that covered the top of the terrarium (exactly the same dimension as the outside dimension of the terrarium, and then cut a second, slightly smaller piece of Plexiglas (narrow enough to fit inside of the terrarium). I then welded the two pieces together, one on top of the other, using the same solvent. This creates a "stacked" piece of acrylic glass that covers the top neatly but won't slide around. Be careful with the amount solvent you use. I used too much, and you can see where there was solvent and where there was not. Just use a little bit, or as an alternative, you could put a heavy-duty glue dot at each corner to hold the pieces together. (Glue dots are adhesive dots sold in rolls at craft stores.)

8. NOW comes the fun part. You get to fill it up! Follow the same "recipe" as the small terrariums on page 14. Add gravel, activated carbon, peat moss, soil, and plants. Check out the sources section at the back of the book to learn where I buy my plants.

9. BUILD a basic box for the base of the terrarium, with the sides made out of ⅛-inch plywood and the bottom built from ¾-inch MDF. The bottom of the base needs to be thick enough for the screws that will attach the legs. Nail it together, putty it, sand it, and stain it.

tip:

After you are finished, use a heat gun to polish the sanded edges so they are clear and shiny instead of sanded and dull. Polish only the edges that didn't get glued.

supply list:

- bowl of your choice
- diamond drill bit
- drill
- spray bottle

turning a bowl into a planter

I f you find something fabulous at a thrift store, yard sale or antique store that would fit right in with your existing decor, but it doesn't have a drainage hole, no problem! It is easier that you might think to add one. You just need to make sure you have the right tools.

Watch out! Once you know how to add a drainage hole, you may just be tempted to grab bowls out of your cabinet and turn them into planters.

"Where the large mixing bowl, honey?"

"It's in the front room with a fern in it, dear!"

Choose a bowl deep enough for the plant that will be making the bowl its home. I suggest searching flea markets, thrift stores, and your favorite home decor store to find good prices. Once you know you can turn almost anything into a planter, ideas for creative new planters will start to jump out at you.

You will need a drill with a diamond tip bit. The bit I bought was about ten dollars, and it made a half-inch hole. You will also need a way to keep the bottom of the bowl wet while you are drilling. I use a spray bottle. Keeping water handy will help you keep the drill bit cool, which is important since friction from drilling will create heat and melt the glue that is holding the diamonds onto the drill bit. If you want your drill bit to last, water will help keep it cool and extend its life so you can use it over and over to make more beautiful planters!

1. START by making a notch in the bowl. The surface is smooth and therefore slippery. If you turn the drill bit on an angle and drill just long enough to create a notch, it will make it easier to drill the rest of the hole.

2. ONCE you have the notch, continue drilling on an angle. While drilling, slowly bring the drill upright until you are drilling straight down. Use some pressure (but not too much force) as you drill.

3. WHEN you get close to drilling all the way through, you will feel a difference in how the drill feels in your hands. You need to anticipate it breaking through by not pushing as hard on the drill. Make sure the drill doesn't slam into the bottom of the bowl when the drill bit finally goes through. I tighten up my upper body to create more control over where the drill is going.

It really is that easy to add a drainage hole to something ceramic or glass. Think of all the possibilities!

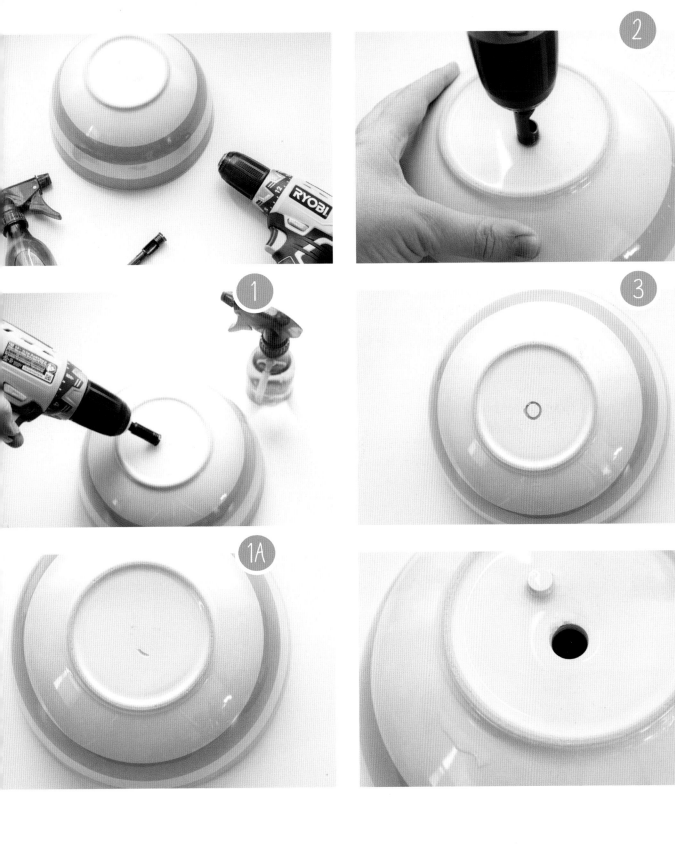

supply list:

- measuring tape
- 1 × 1 or ¾-inch square dowels
- compound miter saw
- nail gun
- wood glue
- wood putty
- 220-grit sandpaper
- foam brush

- stain or paint of your choice
- wire
- potted plant
- ceiling hook

geometric hanging planter

I had a plan. A plan to make the most amazing hanging geometric planter. But I stink at math. Enter my husband. I told him how I wanted this planter to look. I even gave him a drawing. Then he figured out the angles and how I should cut it on the miter saw. So this project comes to you courtesy of me and my better half.

GO VERTICAL

When you have a small space, going vertical with storage is the best thing you can do to free up room on the floor. Even if you don't have a small space, going vertical adds visual interest. Whether you are hanging it from the ceiling, adding it to a shelf, or mounting it to the wall, going vertical is also a fun way to display your plants.

I love almost every kind of hanging planter. I have hesitated to have anything hanging in my home because, well, I live with four young boys. I figured if they literally swing from the chandeliers, then a hanging planter might not be the best idea. But they are getting older, and I can now have a few nice things without fear they will get ruined. So I decided to go for it, and this is what I came up with.

You will need some 1 × 1 or ¾-inch square dowels. They are sold with the regular dowels in your home improvement store. Cut eight dowels into eleven-inch lengths. Once they are cut to length, you will need to cut several angle cuts. I took a lot of pictures of each step, and because of all the pictures, it looks more complicated than it really is. Don't be intimidated!

1. TURN your miter saw to 45°. Find the center of the 1 × 1 and mark it. You will only be cutting from the halfway mark.

2. CUT one side as shown. Flip the 1 × 1 over and cut the other side, creating a point like a fence picket.

3. TURN the 1 × 1 on its side.

4. THE miter saw is already set at 45° on the front, but you will now need to turn you saw to 45° again (compound cut) by turning the dial on the back.

5. MAKE the next cut.

6. MOVE the 1 × 1 to its other side to make the next cut and turn it over.

7. NOW you need to cut the other end of each 1 × 1 dowel. It is just one simple cut. Go ahead and change the back dial on the miter saw so it is back to 0°. The front dial will still be set to 45°.

8. MAKE a simple 45° cut. Make sure you cut it on the correct side.

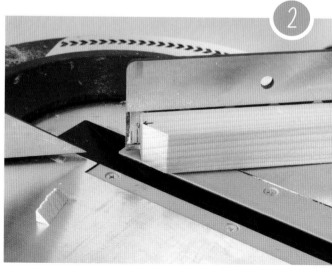

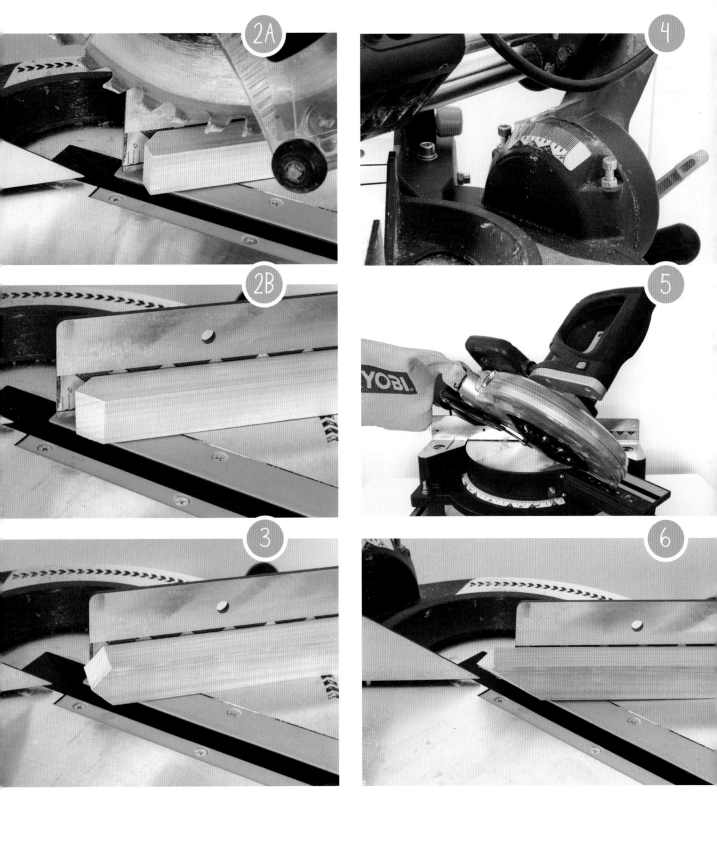

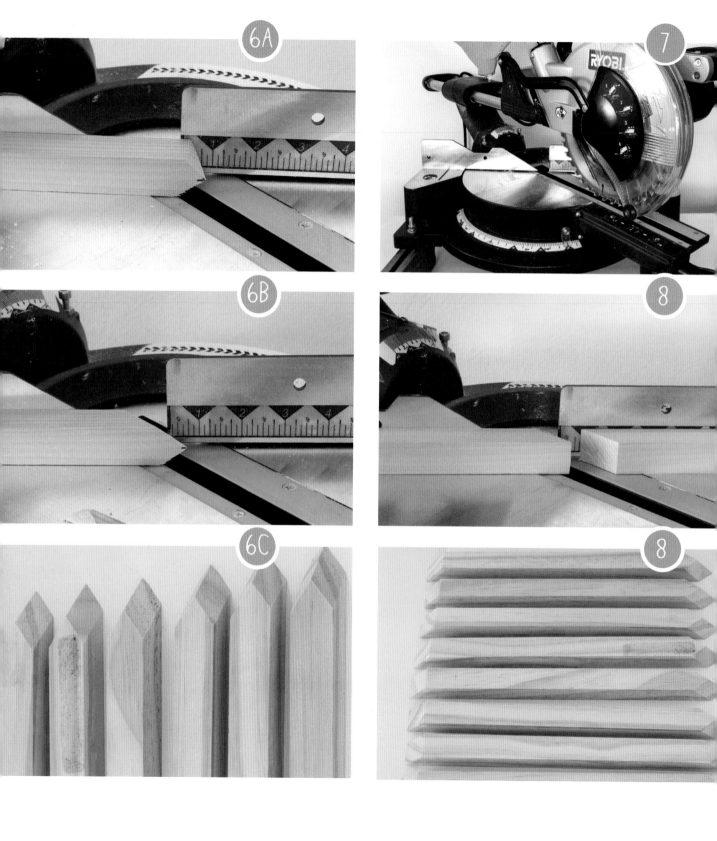

Whew! Are you still with me? I know that seemed like a lot of steps. We are ready to assemble though. Almost done!

9. NAIL these pieces together with the help of a second person. I tried to do it alone and got frustrated. One person can hold it together, and the other can nail. You will nail together the compound mitered edged first, which will form a point. I did it two pieces at a time and then nailed those two sets of two together. I knew I was going to be drilling a hole through the top for the wire, so I was careful at what angle I shot the nails through so the nails wouldn't be in the way when I drilled.

10. ONCE you have the two halves nailed together in their mitered points, you can nail them together.

11. PUTTY, sand, and stain the constructed shape. Remember that if you are going to be staining, use a putty that is stainable and sandable. Also, choose a putty that is close to the color you will be staining. Overfill the nail holes and sand smooth when it is dry.

To hang it, wrap and twist a wire on each side of the pot. If you have a larger pot, you may need more wires. Feed the wires through a hole drilled in the top of the wood, and twist those wires together too. Hang it from a ceiling hook by wrapping the wire around it tightly. All the weight should be held by the wire and not the geometric shape. You can choose to hang it using other ways as well. Maybe with a chain?

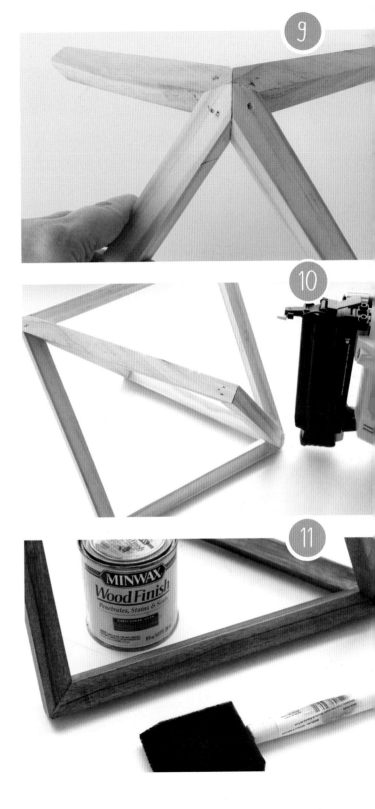

supply list:

supply list:

- polymer clay
- kitchen oven
- paint (optional)
- string, rope, twine, or chain

hanging clay planter

Do you remember playing with play dough as a kid? I made birds' nests filled with play dough eggs until after my first pottery lesson in middle school art class. From then on, I was hooked on making pots. Playing with clay is just as fun as an adult. And you can make useful (and pretty) things too.

My clay of choice is usually polymer clay. It doesn't dry out, and when you bake it in your oven, it becomes quite hard and waterproof, which is perfect for this project.

You can make this planter as big or as small as you would like. I chose to make a small one—perfect for a succulent. Sculpt the clay into a bowl. I don't worry about the shape being perfect. I think the imperfections make it special and give it the handmade look I like.

1. ONCE you have a bowl-shaped pot (or whatever shape you want) you will need to add a drainage hole and a hole on each side to thread rope or twine through later. If you are making a larger planter, I would make three or four holes to hang it with.

2. JUST as you have endless possibilities for the color, shape, and size of your pot, you also have unlimited ways to decorate it. I used a flat head screwdriver to make little *x*'s all over. I also considered rolling it over burlap to give it some fun texture or using a butter knife to create lines. Use your imagination!

3. PUT it in the oven after you finish your design. Place it on an oven-safe plate and bake it at 275°F. Follow the directions on the packaging for the correct time and temperature for the brand of clay you are using. After it has cooled, you can either plant your plant immediately or paint your pot. I painted the inside of the *x*'s and used a wet wipe to clean off any paint that got outside the lines. Because the design was below the surface, I could wipe it off without affecting the paint inside the design.

4. ADD the twine, rope, or chain of your choice, and put a little plant inside. Make multiple planters, and hang them together in a group or one large one above a side table.

supply list:

- measuring tape
- 1 × 6 boards (18)
- miter saw
- table saw
- wood glue
- nail gun
- pencil
- drill with large drill bit
- plywood or 1-inch laminate pine board

- jig saw
- wood putty
- 220-grit sandpaper
- foam brush
- paint or stain

hexagon planter

C an't find what you like at the store? Or maybe the space where you want to put a planter has unique measurements? Then make your own! It is fun to customize your planters. I have several ideas to share.

I love geometric shapes, and I think the hexagon is my favorite. I see them all the time in the design world. I knew I had to include them somewhere in this book. So why not three gold hexagon planters?

These are larger and meant to sit on the floor. If you want to make them smaller to put them on a surface, such as a counter or side table, you can use smaller boards.

I used 1 × 6 boards to build these planters. Each planter had six boards for the six sides. One planter is eight inches high, one is thirteen inches high, and the tallest is eighteen inches high.

I have a sliding compound miter saw, so I can cut a 1 × 6 with it. If you have a non-sliding miter saw, you will either have to cut most of it and then turn it around to cut the remaining bit, or use a table saw. I recommend the table saw because you will get a cleaner line than trying to cut it twice with the miter saw.

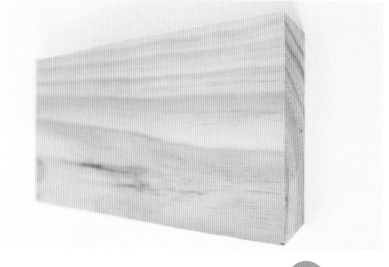

1. ONCE you have the boards cut to length, you will need to make an angled cut on each of the long sides. You will do this by adjusting the blade on your table saw. Set your blade to 30°.

2. ONCE you have all your boards cut, it is time to attach them together.

3. ADD wood glue to one of the long edges. Do not put too much on, or it will ooze out when nailed together. A thin, even coat is best.

4. ATTACH the two sides using a brad nailer. Be careful at which angle you are directing the nail gun to make sure the nail goes in at the angle you want. Attach remaining sides together.

5. CREATE a bottom for the planter by setting the newly constructed planter onto a board and tracing the inside.

6. USE a jigsaw to cut the traced shape out.

7. DRILL some holes in the bottom for proper drainage.

Since these planters would go in my living room on the hardwood floors, I didn't want them leaking on to the floor every time I watered them. I decided to attach the bottom higher into the planter instead of on the very bottom. This way I could add a bowl under it to catch the runoff. I placed the bowl I would use under it to make sure there was enough clearance. Then I nailed the bottom board into place.

8. AFTER it is all assembled, fill the nail holes with putty. Overfill the holes.

9. ONCE the putty dries, sand it smooth. I chose a metallic paint. Since shiny metallic anything shows every little flaw, I sanded like crazy to get it as smooth as possible. I love how they turned out and can't wait to find them a permanent spot in my living room.

7

7A

tip:

tip:

If you will be staining, chose a putty that is stainable, paintable, and sandable. Make sure it is a color that is close to the color you will be staining the piece. It says stainable, but the putty will only stain to a point. A light putty will not stain as dark as you need for a walnut stain.

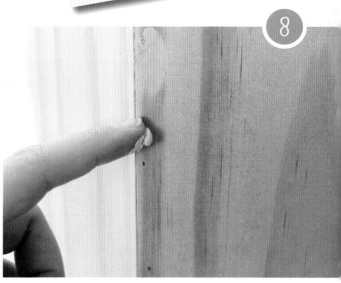

8

9

supply list:

- measuring tape
- 16 feet of 1 × 4 boards
- miter saw
- Kreg Jig
- screws
- jigsaw
- nail gun
- putty
- 220-grit sandpaper
- plywood for bottom
- foam brush
- stain or paint

crate planter

The very first piece of furniture I ever built from scratch was a storage crate. I am not sure what it is about crates, but I love them, so I had to include a tutorial. You can rough it up and make it more rustic or have it sleek and smooth for a more contemporary look.

1. FIRST, I had to decide how big I wanted the crate to be. I cut 1 × 4 boards with a miter saw, then cut them all into twelve-inch lengths. I didn't care if the crate was exactly square, so this worked for me. (Note: If you want it to be exactly 12 × 12 inches, then you would have to cut half of the boards shorter to fit inside the twelve-inch boards. I measure two boards together, and whatever I get is the dimension I subtract from the length of the boards to make them shorter.)

2. ONCE they have been cut to length, I use the Kreg Jig to create pocket holes (see the X Planter on page 45 for more details). I gave half of the boards pocket holes on the ends so they could connect at the corners and the other half pocket holes more in the middle (going the other direction) to connect each layer together.

3. GRAB one board that has the pocket holes on the end and one that doesn't, and attach them.

tip:

Sanding the boards before you assemble them will make the seams stand out more.

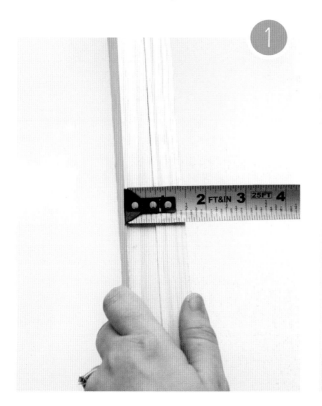

4. REPEAT until you make your first square.

5. THIS is when the pocket holes that are facing the other direction (more towards the middle) come in handy. You will screw all the square "frames" together using those pocket holes.

6. CREATE a bottom using the technique described in the Hexagon Planter tutorial (see page 33) by setting the crate onto a sheet of plywood and tracing the inside. Cut it out with a jigsaw, and nail it into place with a brad nailer.

Make sure to remember to drill a drainage hole or holes in the bottom as well.

7. PUTTY over the nail holes with a sandable, stainable, paintable putty that closely matches the color you will be staining. Overfill and sand it smooth when it has completely dried.

8. YOU are ready to stain or paint your crate! I chose a gray color, but the choices of finishes and colors are endless. Choose something based on your existing decor so it fits right in.

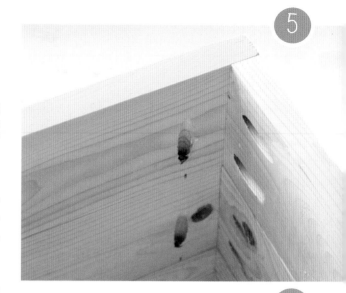

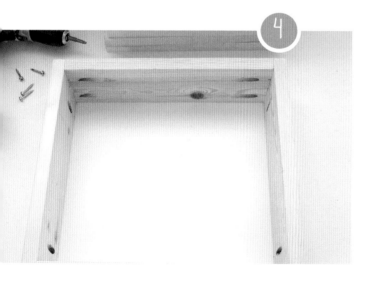

Another way you could build this crate planter without using a Kreg Jig would be to use 1 × 1 boards in the corners to attach the other boards together. This is how I built my first crate.

supply list:

- terracotta pots
- primer
- waterproof sealer
- paint
- painter's tape
- foam brush

painting pots

Terracotta pots are inexpensive, readily available, and easily customizable. But they are porous, and you can't just slap a coat of paint on them and expect it to last. I'll show you how I paint pots to make them last longer.

Make sure your pots are clean. I usually scrub them really well in warm water and let them dry if they are new. If they are old and have lots of dirt, you will need to use soap (but not too much), and make sure you rinse it all off.

1. START with a great bonding primer on the outside of the pot. A paint job is only as good as the prep work, and in this case that is the cleaning and the primer.

2. SEAL the inside of the pot to make it waterproof. If you don't seal it, when you water the plant, the moisture will seep through the terracotta and damage the paint job. I used Rust-Oleum's Never-Wet two-step product. Any sealer that works for brick or concrete would work.

3. PAINT the pot the color of your choice. I painted mine a creamy white. I wanted to add some gold detail to them, so I measured where I wanted the details to be, and then I taped off the design.

4. THERE is a trick I use when I need really crisp lines. I paint a layer of the base coat over the tape first. Once it is dry (and has sealed the tape), I paint the top color. You will get the nicest lines every single time. Also, remove the tape before the paint has dried so you don't risk the paint coming off with the tape.

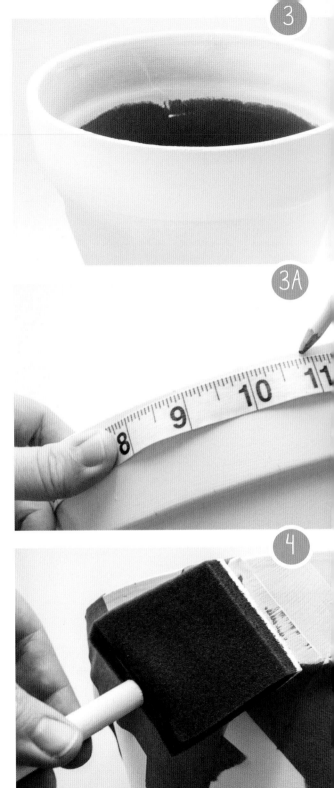

supply list:

- measuring tape or carpenter's square
- ½-inch sheet of plywood (4 × 8)
- 36 feet of 1 × 3 boards
- miter saw
- table saw
- nail gun
- Kreg Jig
- drill

- screws
- putty
- foam brush
- paint or stain

x planter

I love just about anything with an *x* detail, so when I bought a lemon tree that required a larger planter box than what I currently had on hand, I knew I would make one with *x*'s on it! This project can be modified to any size. Instead of 1 × 3 boards, you could use lattice molding or 1 × 2s for the trim if you want a smaller planter.

1. CUT four squares out of plywood. I made mine an eighteen-inch square.

2. CUT the 1 × 3s to eighteen inches long. After you have sixteen boards cut to length, you will need to cut the ends at a 45° angle.

3. NAIL the trim onto the plywood around the edges to create a border.

4. NEXT, you will need more 1 × 3 boards. I put the 1 × 3 board up to the corner of the border and traced it so I knew where to cut so the 1 × 3 would fit snugly into the corner.

Cut eight boards this way. Then, after attaching one to each side, cut the other four to fit inside to complete the *x*.

5. WHEN they are all cut and nailed into place, putty the nail holes and any seams or knotholes. If you plan on staining, remember to choose a putty that is stainable and is close in color to the stain you will be using. Use a foam brush to apply the paint or stain.

6. ONCE you have four panels with the *x* detail in place, take them to the table saw and cut a 45° angle along the two parallel side edges. Refer to the picture in the Hexagon Planter tutorial (see page 33 to learn more about angle cutting.

7. USE a Kreg Jig to attach the sides together. Drill pocket holes on two of the panels.

8. SCREW them together.

9. MAKE a bottom once the sides are all connected. Use the same method shown in the Hexagon Planter tutorial (see page 33). Trace the bottom onto plywood, cut it out, and then nail it in. Putty those holes, and you are ready to paint or stain it!

However you display these planters, I hope you add more houseplants to your home. I really believe it will improve your life and elevate your decor!

tip:

For the most accurate fit, measure and cut each board individually.

⑦

⑧

ANOTHER WAY

ANOTHER WAY

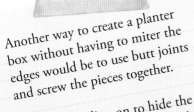

Another way to create a planter box without having to miter the edges would be to use butt joints and screw the pieces together.

Nail the molding on to hide the screws. If you miter the trim, the corner will be seamless. But I have done it without mitering too.

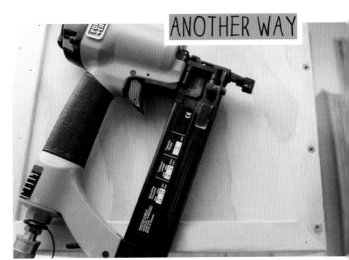

I t is not enough merely to exist. . . . [You] need freedom, sunshine, and a little flower for a companion.[1]

–Hans Christian Andersen

chapter 3: flowers

Before we jump into how to decorate with flowers, I want to discuss how to keep your cut flowers looking their best for as long as possible. If you are going to the effort of using them in your home, and if they cheer you up like they do me, then you want them to last as long as possible.

HOW TO CARE FOR CUT FLOWERS

I plant a lot of flowers in my yard. I do it partly for the curb appeal but mostly because I like to cut them and bring them inside. In the winter, I treat myself to some inexpensive grocery store flowers once a week or so. It helps get me through the tough Utah winters.

Before I cut or buy flowers, I try to remember to wash out the vase really well. Bacteria are the enemy and will make your flowers die off more quickly. I use either hot soapy water or a little bleach water.

I try to cut the flowers in my yard in the morning when it is cool. The cool temperatures and the dew help the petals and leaves stay hydrated. If you pick flowers during the heat of the day when they are slightly wilted, they won't last as long.

Once I bring them inside, I cut them with something sharp (clippers or scissors) at an angle while holding the stem under water. You'll need to do this even if you purchase cut flowers from a florist. Holding the stem under water as you cut it keeps air bubbles out of the stem, extending the life of the flower. If you tear the stem or cut it with something dull, it will affect how long your flowers last. Cutting on an angle gives the bottom of the stem more surface area and allows it to suck up more water. I pull off the bottom leaves next. Any leaves that sit in the water will rot quickly, making the water cloudy and sticky while also decreasing the life of the flowers.

When the leaves are stripped off from the bottom of the stems, I rinse the stems off in lukewarm water before putting them in the vase. I like very simple arrangements. Most of the time I put a single type of flower in a vase. And if I do add more than one kind of flower, I do it in a random, no-fuss way. But you can arrange them any way you like.

As far as food goes, most of the time I use plain water. If I buy them at the store or from a florist, then I add the flower food that is sometimes packaged with the flowers. I have not used anything else. I have heard from other gardeners that homemade concoctions (aspirin, vinegar, sugar, bleach, and mouthwash) do not work, so I have not tested them out myself. The sugar is thought to be food and the others are added to kill off bacteria, which we talked about earlier. I think if you have clean water and a clean vase, you are fine. The one trick I have tried is adding a penny. I think it was one of my blog readers who first suggested it to me. I had some tulips that were drooping, and she said to try a penny. I did, and they perked back up. I have used that trick with tulips ever since.

Here are a few more dos and don'ts.

Make sure you change the water every couple of days. Steer clear of putting the vase of flowers in direct sun. And don't put them too close to a fruit bowl. Fruit gives off ethylene gas that ripens the fruit but decreases the life of your flowers.

HOW TO DECORATE WITH FLOWERS

You might feel a sense of déjà vu here because a few of these points are the same as the last chapter. Plants and flowers are so similar that it really is not a big surprise that there would be some similarities in how to decorate with them.

Use Unique Items as Vases

The cool thing about vases is that, unlike planters, you don't need to worry about drainage. You can get really creative! Make sure that what you use can be cleaned really well on the inside so the bacteria won't affect your flowers' lifespan. I have a couple of go-to items when it comes to vases, and pitchers are one of them. I *love* how flowers look in a crisp white pitcher!

My mom has a collection of vintage pitchers that are all different colors. Wouldn't they look amazing as centerpieces at a gathering?

Another idea is to use a bucket. I use buckets as planters, but they also make great vases as long as you can clean them well. Steer clear of buckets with rust on the inside, and make sure they are watertight. I like old buckets best because I like the contrast of the dented and worn bucket with the fresh colorful flowers. But a new bucket would be a perfect choice too.

Why not add some small flowers to a shell? It certainly is not your normal vase option!

Use what you already have. Grab a bowl from the cabinet, and make it into a temporary vase.

As with the planters, you can have a lot of fun if you go vertical. Hang them from the ceiling with rope, twine, or ribbon. Just make sure the top of the vase has a lip that the rope can be tied around. Or make a wall-mounted vase out of polymer clay.

The method for a wall-mounted planter is similar to the method for the hanging clay planter described in the previous chapter (see page 30). I just made sure that instead of a round shape, the back was flat. I used a regular sawtooth picture hanger but bent the ends.

Then I pushed it into the clay, leaving a little room between the sawtooth hanger and the clay for the nail to rest. I baked it according to the directions on the package, and when it had cooled, it was ready to hang!

supply list:

- plastic bottles for molds
- pen to trace
- box cutter or razor blade knife
- rapid-set cement
- mixing bowl or bucket
- paint stick or something to stir with
- bud vase (optional)

Can't find what you like at the store? Or maybe the space where you want to put a planter has unique measurements? Then make your own vase or planter! It is fun to customize your planters. I have several ideas to share.

concrete vase

I love the whole idea of a cold gray concrete vase filled with soft, delicate flowers. I also love the idea that concrete, which is considered by many to be very modern and masculine, can be paired with a traditional and even romantic flower. I also just love playing around with concrete!

First you need to think about what shape you want and what to use as your mold. Simple is better since you will have to get it out of the mold. But if your plastic is thin enough to cut with a razor blade knife, you may be able to create a more interesting shape. I prefer simple 90 percent of the time, so I chose a shampoo bottle for the outside and a hair spray bottle for the inside.

1. PREPARE to cut the top off of the larger of the two bottles so the opening is large enough to pour the cement into it. I used a spray paint lid as a template and traced around it.

2. USE the razor blade knife to cut the top off.

3. MIX the cement. I used an old bowl and a paint stick and followed the directions on the package.

4. ONCE it is mixed well, pour it into the bottle, and fill the bottle ¾ of the way full.

5. GRAB the bottle you will use for the center of the vase. I added cooking spray the outside of the bottle like I had seen some people do for shallow concrete planters. This is supposed to help it come out more easily at the end of the project. Make sure the bottle is weighted down, or it will pop back up after you push it into the cement. I added gravel since I had it handy from an earlier project.

6. IF there is still room at the top after pushing the bottle down into the cement, hurry and fill the space before it starts to set. I gently shook it and banged it on the tabletop to make sure the cement settled well. Finally, smooth the top with your finger.

7. LET the cement cure overnight before taking it out of the mold. If it is still warm to the touch (It gets hot during the curing time), then it is not ready yet. Use the razor blade knife to slit both sides, and then just pop the finished vase out. As far as getting out the hair spray bottle from the inside, I had mixed results. One bottle came out

but not without some serious prying. The second bottle wouldn't budge. So I decided to just cut the top section of the hair spray bottle off and call it good. No one is going to see the inside of your vase anyway and it saves you the effort of trying to pry it out.

Another option that I tried was adding a glass bud vase with the intention of just leaving it inside. My large bud vase was very tall, so it had to stick out a bit. I am thinking of finding shorter bud vases and making some more. I have a concrete vase addiction now!

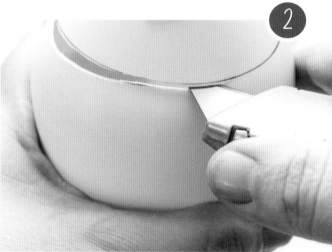

supply list:

- cotton string
- glue that dries clear
- bowl
- paper towels

I bought the next four vases at the dollar store, and I adore their shape! I wanted to show different ways to change them up and personalize them to your individual style. You can re-create these exact projects, or use them as the jumping-off point to make something completely unique.

string vase

For this dollar-store vase, I added some string to the outside. It is easy, albeit messy. Think papier-mâché projects from your elementary school days. But if you are not afraid of getting your hands a little dirty (or in this case sticky), then this is a fun project.

1. CHOOSE a bright-colored cotton string. The cotton will absorb the glue mixture well. Choose a glue that will dry clear. Mix a little water into the glue. You want to thin it slightly but not so that it is watery. Unravel a good amount of string, and add it to the glue.

2. RUN it through your fingers to remove the excess glue.

3. WRAP the string around the vase vertically, horizontally, and diagonally. Make sure you end the string at the bottom. Tuck the end of the string under the vase.

4. ONCE you are done, dab any extra glue with a paper towel.

Let it dry before using it. I put water and flowers in it, and it was fine. But when I went to dump the water out when the flowers had expired, the outside got wet and the string softened a little. This is probably because I didn't use the right type of glue, but this vase would also make a fun decorative vase without flowers. Add some sticks or feathers instead.

supply list:

- vase
- marker
- spray paint
- 3D glass paint or puff paint

monogram vase

I think this next idea would make a great gift and could also be used as a centerpiece for a wedding. Or maybe you would rather use an image rather than monogram letters. You can do just about anything.

1. DECIDE how you want your monogram to look, and draw it on the vase with a sharpie marker. If you mess up, a Magic Eraser will remove the marker easily.

2. USE the 3D glass paint to outline the marker. You could also use puff paint or a thick craft glue.

3. LET it dry completely. Once it has dried, spray-paint it with your choice of color. Try not to get the paint on the inside of the vase. You can go with a matte finish or go glossy like I did. I chose a simple vase shape, but you could do this on just about any vase. You can find them inexpensively at thrift stores and yard sales. If your vase of choice doesn't look fresh and new, no problem! You are going to give it new life.

2

supply list:

• vase

• glass paint

• paper towels

drip vase

This was a fun vase to make! I want to make a million in every color now. It was the quickest one too.

1. USING some glass paint and a pointy top that I "stole" from the top of the 3D paint bottle I used in the Monogram Vase tutorial on page 63, I simply squeezed glass paint along the top of the vase and let it drip down. Have some paper towels handy in case you don't like the pattern. You can just wipe it off and start over. Luckily, mine worked out perfect the first time. Wait the appropriate time for it to dry. Some glass paints (like the one I used) will also need to be baked on a low temperature in your oven.

supply list:

- vase
- electrical tape
- glass etching cream
- small paint brush

glass etched stripe vase

I think once you etch your first piece of glass, you will be hooked. I think you will start going around your house to find things to etch. At least that is how I was. The first thing I ever etched was a glass pitcher. I put our monogram on it. It is still one of my favorite pieces. So when I was thinking of ways to transform the dollar store vase several different ways, etching was a no-brainer.

1. USE electrical tape to make the stripes. If you try to use painter's tape, it will pucker as you try to wrap it straight all the way around. Electrical tape will stretch and go on nice and flat.

2. YOU can purchase glass-etching cream at any craft store. Be careful with it (don't get it in your eyes or on your skin) and read the instructions before using. I used a paintbrush to apply it.

3. ONCE all the cream is on, wait at least sixty seconds to allow the cream to do its thing.

4. RINSE the cream off, and then remove the tape.

You don't have to just do stripes. If you have access to a machine that cuts vinyl, you can cut out just about anything to use as a stencil. If you don't have one, you can use a razor blade knife or order a vinyl cutout online. Custom designs are easy to order online.

supply list:

- log, cut to size
- drill
- bore bit
- bud vase

log vase

A huge tree in our backyard fell over during a storm. We cut the branches and put them in a pile in our back yard, and I have been trying to use them in all sorts of projects so my poor tree gets new life. For example, I use them as candleholders all the time. It only seemed logical to try to make a bud vase with them.

1. USE a bore bit (also called a spade or paddle bit) that is slightly wider than the width of the bud vase. Simply drill down deep enough for the bud vase to fit.

2. SLIP the glass bud vase right in!

supply list:

- copper wire
- bud vase
- pliers or wire snips

copper vase

I love the look of copper, and it is easy to work with too. I knew I had to do something fun with it, and a vase seemed like a good way to use it. I made a few different versions. I hope it inspires you to do this project or come up with a version of your own!

1. BUY some copper wire and a few little bud vases. You can buy copper wire at your home improvement store by the foot.

2. WIND the copper around the bud vase. It was quick and easy to do.

3. USE the snip part of the needle-nose pliers to cut it off.

4. BEND the bottom so it is wider than the rest. This creates a stable base.

My original idea was to make a vase that spelled out something. After experimenting with the spiral spring-like vases, I decided the best way to get the word to stand up was to add a spiral vase to each end. So I started by making a spiral vase and then instead of cutting it off like I did with the other vases, I bent the wire to spell *love* in cursive. Then the last letter continued into another spiral.

I could not ask for more

EVERY ROOM OF THE HOUSE

I think the most common places that people think of putting a vase of flowers are the coffee table and the dining room table. Those are awesome places. But don't feel limited to just those. I am that crazy lady who puts them in every room of the house. I almost always have them in my kitchen. And if they are in the kitchen, it makes sense to just grab a pitcher to put them in. I even put them in the bathroom sometimes! And my favorite place is in the bedroom next to my side of the bed. I love waking up to the smell of fresh flowers. I usually fill my office space with plants and flowers too. I feel less closed in when I have them around me. And of course you can add them to your living spaces. Flowers should not just be for the benefit of company that may be visiting. You should get to enjoy them all year long!

No matter what you put them in and no matter where you get them from, make a commitment right now to have more flowers in your life. They are not just for special occasions. You don't need a special reason to feel uplifted and to beautify your home.

I go to nature to be soothed and healed, and to have my senses put in tune once more.[1]

–John Burroughs

chapter 4: branches, sticks & stumps

I am sure it is no surprise, given that I was a tomboy, that I climbed trees a lot growing up. I think trees are magnificent. I feel like I am in the presence of God when I am in the mountains and surrounded by trees. In fact, I made several trips up the canyon to sit and be inspired at the beginning of this writing process.

This chapter is full of projects using branches, sticks, and stumps, but I don't think you should chop down a perfectly good tree to decorate your home. There are enough routine trimmings that need to be done that you'll never lack for wood sources once you know where to find them. We had a big beautiful tree fall during a huge storm a few years ago. I was devastated. Instead of using it all for firewood, I vowed to use as much of it as I could in projects for my home. Many of the wood projects in this book have been created using wood from that fallen giant, as well as trimmings from our yard and my mom's yard.

supply list:

- chain saw
- table saw
- paint, epoxy
- wood screws and drill
- putty (optional)

white-and-gold tree stump side table

When looking through our pile of tree limbs and stumps. I saw a section that had a thick stump that branched out into three "legs." The first thing I thought of was that it looked like a table base. So I used the chainsaw to make it roughly the size I wanted and then cut it more accurately with a table saw.

My base was pretty stable, but I want to tell you how you could add another leg if you needed to. Maybe you have a branch with only two "legs," and you want to add a third. Simply cut a branch that is similar in size as the other ones. Then cut it at an angle as if it had grown out of the tree originally. I used long wood screws to attach it and then puttied over them. Normally, you would want to sand putty smooth, but in this case, the rougher the better! It will just look like the bark. And since I painted it, no one could even tell the difference. If you don't want to paint yours, use a putty that closely resembles the bark. Then have that side be the back of the table so it is less noticeable.

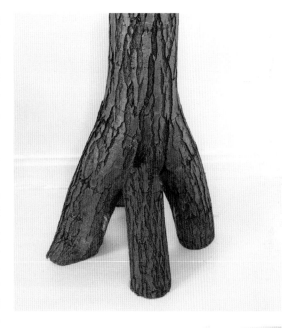

For the top, I just bought a round piece of wood at Home Depot. It was around seven dollars. I spray-painted it gold and let it dry for a few days before attaching to the base. For some reason, metallic spray paint seems to need a little more cure time.

I used heavy-duty glue to attach the top to the base. I love how it came out!

stump entry table

Here is another table that I made using tree stumps. I cut the stumps to the same height and then added a faux live edge top using heavy-duty glue. For the live edge top, I bought a twelve-inch-wide board. I angled the blade on my jigsaw and cut a wiggly line along one edge. I sanded it really well and stained it. If you wanted a wider table, add a larger tabletop and four legs instead of two. You could also make shorter legs and use it as a coffee table!

stump crayon holder

I originally made this to show how you could use it to store your makeup brushes, but then I made a kid's desk (later in this chapter), and this just seemed like a perfect fit for the desk, so I added crayons and paint brushes. You could use it for so many things!

I simply cut it to the height I wanted and then drilled holes in the top. Drill the holes slightly bigger than what you intend to store in there. Because of the weathered look of the wood, I left it as it was but you can seal it with polyurethane as well.

supply list:

- tree stump
- saw
- drill
- drill bit
- floating shelf bracket
- screws
- polyurethane (optional)

tree stump shelf

I can't remember where I was, but I remember seeing a chunk of wood hanging on a wall. Maybe it was a restaurant or an antique shop. It didn't have anything on it, but it stuck out pretty far and it gave me the idea for this shelf. I only had two stump sections that still had bark on them, and I used them for other projects, so I actually bought this tree stump slice from a store. But if I had another section of my poor wind-fallen tree, I would have sanded the chainsaw marks down and used it. I could have used a section of tree stump that didn't have bark as well, but sometimes I get a vision in my mind, and I have to have it that way. Anyone else like that?

1. CUT the stump in half.

2. BUY a floating shelf bracket. I bought mine online. They have steel rods with a back plate that you screw into the wall. The shelf just slides right on. To use this type of bracket, drill some holes for the brackets to fit into. Use a drill bit that is slightly bigger than the bracket so it has room to slide in. Drill as straight as you can.

3. SLIDE the bracket into the hole just a little bit. I held it up to the wall where I wanted it to go and marked where the screw holes needed to be.

4. ONCE the brackets are screwed into the wall, you can slide the shelf back on.

supply list:

supply list:

- tree stump
- bore bit
- really strong arms
- drill and large drill bit
- sealer
- foam brush
- hairpin legs (optional)

tree stump planter

When we lost our backyard tree to a windstorm, we cut several chunks of the trunk into smaller sections. I left some of those stumps in the backyard over the winter and some stored in my garage. The ones in the garage kept their bark on, but the ones outside lost the bark, revealing a unique pattern underneath. I decided to hollow one out and make a planter.

tip:

Stumps need time to dry out before you can use them. The time required to dry out depends on where you live and your humidity levels. If you live somewhere humid, I have heard it can take as long as a year. Another option would be to use a kiln or your oven on a very low temperature to dry it out.

1. USE a bore bit (also known as a spade bit or paddle bit) to hollow out your chosen tree stump.

2. HOLLOWING it out is a long and tedious process. I got about halfway, and my arms begged me to let my husband take over. It took a few days of taking turns before it was deep enough for my liking.

3. ONCE it is hollowed out, drill a large drainage hole in the bottom, and apply sealer to the inside. (I like Helmsman sealer made by Minwax).

4. ONCE it is dry, add three four-inch hairpin legs to create a modern tree stump planter.

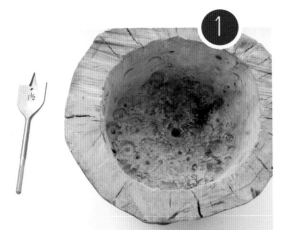

supply list:

- branch
- large bore bit
- drill
- candles
- succulent plant

log and succulent candle holder

Inspiration for DIY nature projects will come from almost anywhere once you get started. I think that's a reflection of a human being's natural instinct to want to connect with nature. When we moved into our home, we were excited to see that the previous owners had installed a backyard fire pit and already had a small supply of firewood nearby. The pile included a log that had weathered to a nice gray color. It also had termite or some kind of insect trails all over it. It was gorgeous! I knew I wanted to do something with it other than burn it in the fire. So I stuck it in the garage to save it for when inspiration struck.

I couldn't make up my mind about whether it should be a succulent planter or a candlestick, so I finally just combined the two!

1. START by scrubbing the log clean. Let it dry. I needed the hole for the plant to be as big as possible so that there would be room for the plant, so I got the largest bore bit I could find (also known as a paddle or spade bit) and drilled a deep hole.

2. CHOOSE a drill bit that is slightly wider in diameter than the candles for the candle holes.

I think sometimes we think of home decor as permanent items. It is okay, especially when decorating with things from nature, to have decor be temporary or have the ability to transition with the seasons. This project is an example of that. I picked a plant at Home Depot that had a very small pot so I knew that it would fit into the hole I had created. I knew it wouldn't live in that small space forever and that it would need to be repotted later, but I could enjoy it in the meantime. I ended up keeping it for a couple of months before finding my little plant a new home in a larger pot. This would be stunning as a table centerpiece or on an entry table for the summer. Later, you can switch it out with something else. I like to rotate my decor. It makes me feel like my house is always new and fresh.

supply list:

• miter saw

• branch

• epoxy

• screws

• polyurethane to seal (optional)

wood slice drawer pulls

I kind of have a wood slice obsession. I love that you see the bark and all of the tree rings. I think wood grain is sexy. I tried to think of as many wood slice projects as possible, so visit my blog at notjustahousewife.net for more ideas. This wood slice project is so easy! And it adds a fun detail to this regular white dresser.

1. **USE** the miter saw and cut off a small section of the branch. The branches I used had been inside for a long time and had sufficiently dried out. I don't recommend using newly cut branches for this.

2. **AFTER** they are cut, use two-part epoxy to attach screws to the back of them.

The epoxy sets up rather quickly, but I let it sit for a day to fully cure. After those were dry, they were ready to screw into the dresser!

candle stick

As you can see on the dresser, there is a tree branch that I use as a candle holder. You can drill a hole in the top using a bore drill bit so a candle will fit down inside. It is a super easy project and adds so much to a room!

coat tree

This is so easy to do! You just need to find a long branch that has a lot of smaller branches coming off of it. Once it is all trimmed down, simply glue and screw it (from the bottom) into a base with a few long wood screws. I used one-inch-thick pine board cut in a square for the base. You could definitely get more elaborate and creative when it comes to the base.

side table

Gather a bunch of thick branches, and cut them all the same length. Group them together and add a Plexiglas or tempered beveled glass top so you can see the branches. You can use wood glue or screws to keep the branches together.

supply list:

- miter saw (if you are cutting your own wood slices)
- sandpaper
- wood slices
- sealer

drink coasters

Here is another tree slice project! I just love them. And if you buy presliced and presanded ones from a craft store, it doesn't get much easier than this project. But you can also cut your own from a branch or log using a miter saw.

Once you have your slices, all you need to do is seal them. The first coat will absorb almost entirely into the wood. Wait for it to dry and add another coat. I recommend applying three coats.

pot rack

Do you need a pot rack above your kitchen island? Why not just use a branch and some rope? I just slipped on some S hooks and it was ready to go!

kid desk

I was lucky and found two branches that were the same size and both had a Y shape. I was originally going to make an entry table with them. I like using shelves mounted the same height as a table for an entryway table. I made one that way, not out of branches but with shelf brackets, in our first apartment fifteen years ago, and I still like the look. But we had this little green child's chair, so I changed my mind and made it into a child's desk paired with the little green chair.

supply list:

- branch cutters
- sticks
- lampshade
- hot glue gun
- spray paint (optional)

stick lampshade

A couple of my boys went through a phase when they were toddlers where they would collect sticks every single time we went outside. I had piles of sticks all over the house because, of course, they were special "treasures." In fact, when we moved to Las Vegas, Nevada, for a while, my then 2½-year-old cried and cried because there weren't any sticks. My sister sent him a package full of sticks so he could have a collection! So when I see sticks, they make me smile. But I also think they have great texture and can be used in so many ways.

We trimmed our willow trees and had lots of small branches loaded with sticks. I cut them all down to nine inches long. I needed sticks for the table runner as well (which you will see later), so my husband helped. Yep. That is what our Friday nights look like sometimes . . . sitting on the sofa, cutting sticks.

1. CUT the sticks to the length you need, and glue them onto the shade with a hot glue gun.

2. YOU will see the lampshade material through the gaps in the sticks, so you might want to buy one like mine—brownish with a textured pattern.

3. FEEL free to jazz it up any way you like. When I was done with this project, I decided to spray paint it. It gives it a whole new feel, and it still has great texture.

stick shelf

I bought these neat shelf brackets that are meant to sandwich a board. But why not add some sticks or branches in there instead? Make sure you get sticks that are as straight as possible and that they are not too big to fit into the bracket.

supply list:

- sticks
- branch cutters
- natural-colored ribbon
- hot glue gun

stick table runner

Just like with the stick lampshade, I needed a ton of small sticks—enough to lay side by side and have the runner extend for four feet. Good thing my table is on the small side! I cut the sticks nine inches wide, since that was the same size as was needed for the shade. I was on a roll with cutting nine-inchers already, so why stop?

Once they were all cut, I laid out all the sticks how I wanted them. I tried to mix up the different shades of brown, orange, and green. Then I cut two pieces of ribbon the same length I wanted the finished runner to be. I added hot glue to the ribbon and laid it down on the sticks. I did about a four-inch section at a time.

No matter how you use them, the texture of the bark, the patterns of the wood grain, and the unique growing patterns of the branches make for unique home decor!

L ook deep into nature, and then you will understand everything better."

—Unknown

chapter 5: rocks and minerals

I am willing to bet that bringing rocks inside is not the first thing you think of when you when you hear the words *interior decorating*. Those of you with children may have even gotten upset when your kids brought rocks inside, touting them as treasures. I get it (sort of, since I was one of those kids once). They are dirty and common. But they are also beautiful and interesting. And after this chapter, you may just be asking your children to go find rocks for you!

Using rocks can be as simple as adding them to a vignette, a shelf, or bookcase. Or you can make a full-on projects with them. Here are just a few ideas!

supply list:

- 3 feet of 1 × 6 boards
- saw
- sandpaper
- wood glue
- nail gun
- putty
- foam brush
- stain or paint
- sealer
- epoxy
- rocks

rock bookends

Bookends are a recent love of mine. We have had all of our books in boxes in the basement because we haven't had any bookshelves. I am thinking of hanging more floating shelves in my office to accommodate our books, so I made some bookends. As far as woodworking goes, this is a very simple project. If you are new to woodworking, this is a perfect project to start with, and it's a great project for a child to help with as well. And even if you have been woodworking for a long time, it is still a project worth doing. There are so many possibilities as far as the finish and what you add to a bookend, it will give you an opportunity to get your creative juices flowing on a rainy weekend at home.

1. CUT a 1 × 6 board into four pieces: two pieces five inches long and two ten inches long.

2. REMOVE the stickers and sand the ends really well. If there is residue from any stickers, you will have to sand it completely off or your stain won't absorb well in that area.

3. GLUE and then nail the boards together with a brad nailer. Wipe off any glue that may have oozed out with a damp rag. If there is glue on the wood and it dries, the stain won't be able to absorb in those areas, and it will ruin your finish.

4. FILL the nail holes with stainable, sandable putty. I made the mistake of grabbing putty I had used on a previous project, and it was too light. I try to use a putty that is close to the same color as the stain I will use. If that happens to you, and you are stubborn like me and you don't want to change you stain choice, then sand it a lot when you sand it smooth. Sand it so only the small speck that is covering the tiny nail hole is left. You can either leave it like that and it will be less noticeable, or you can add some of the correct putty color over the top to cover it up.

5. NOW it is time to stain. I like to use a foam brush to apply the stain. I apply it generously but not so much that it runs everywhere. Let it sit for a bit before wiping off the excess with paper towels. Then let it dry. If it is not as dark as you would like, apply a second coat of stain. After the stain is dry, you can seal it. My number one choice is polyurethane.

You will need to use epoxy to adhere the rock to the wood. I chose an everyday regular rock from my yard instead of a crystal or geode because I wanted to show that any rock can be a beautiful addition to your decor . . . even the ones your kids dig up out back!

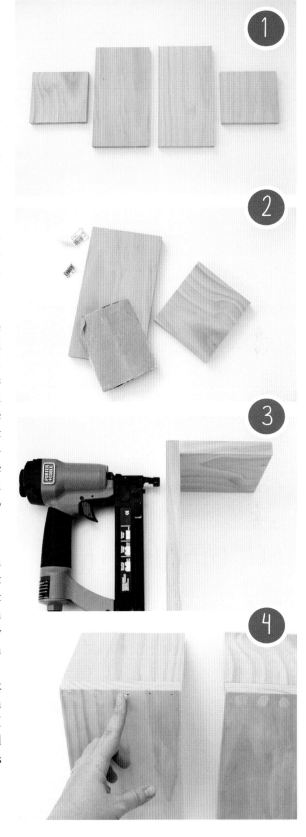

rock candlesticks

Sometimes I randomly have a candlelit dinner, served on real plates, with soft music playing in the background. I do it because sometimes my four boys need a gentle reminder that we don't live in a barn. It is nice to brush up on manners. You know, no elbows on the table, chew with your mouth closed, and no potty humor. You're welcome, my future daughters-in-law.

Over the years, I have collected and made quite a few candleholders. I have a feeling that my rock-collecting boys are going to be huge fans of these. I might have to throw one of my special dinners very soon.

The most important thing for this project is to find rocks that are flat. The flatter the better. The very bottom rock and the top rock are the ones that need to be the most flat of all. If your candlestick is not stable, it can be a big problem.

1. DRY stack your rocks to see if they pass the stability test. If you can stack them up like blocks and they don't fall over, then you are good to go.

2. USE two-part epoxy to adhere the rocks. Mix it well, and add enough glue to each rock that it will have a strong bond over a large surface area but not so much that it runs down the side.

3. GLUE two rocks together, and let them set up before gluing another on top. If you try to glue more than two at a time, the weight from the third rock will make them slip.

Continue this process until you have them the height that you would like. I made four that were varying heights. You can make a tall matching pair or a ton of short ones. It is all up to you!

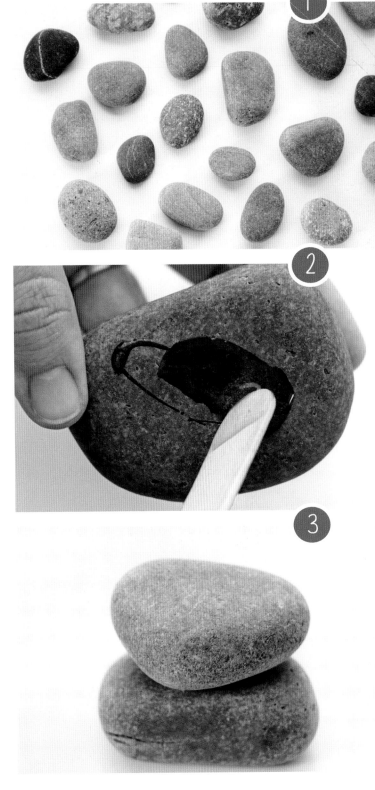

supply list:

- four-inch screws
- epoxy
- rocks
- ½-inch metal pipe
- pipe cutters

rock hooks

I am planning on redecorating my boys' room, and I have been tossing around all sorts of nature-inspired ideas since they would all camp in the mountains 100 percent of their lives if they could. That is how I came up with this next idea. Rock hooks!

1. YOU will need to get some heavy-duty four-inch screws for this projects.

2. USE two-part epoxy to attach the screw to the rock. Only use enough to adhere the screw. You don't want to add too much or it will run all over.

3. TO make it easier to hang things on the rocks, these hooks will need to stick out a ways from the wall. I decided to add some metal pipe for added length. I trimmed it using pipe cutters.

4. WHEN you prepare to attach the rock hook to the wall, simply slip the pipe over the screw. Then screw it into the wall (into a stud).

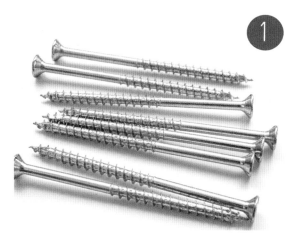

supply list:

- screws
- geodes
- epoxy
- gold paint
- small paint brush

geode drawer pulls

I have been fascinated with geodes since I was a child. I collected, among other things, rocks. A friend of my dad's gave me my first geode and explained that before it is broken open, it looks like an average rock, but if you crack it open, you expose the stunning crystals inside. You can buy them online inexpensively. They are usually called "break your own geodes." You do have to be careful when breaking them open. Use a rag to cover your geode and hit it gently with a hammer. Some will break more easily than others. Buy more than you need because some will not have many crystals, and some will have a thin wall and shatter. The ones that didn't work for this project I gave to my boys to add to their rock collections. They were thrilled.

1. AFTER you have broken your geodes open and washed them really well, use epoxy and add a screw to the back of the rock. I used gold screws since I was going to be painting part of them gold.

2. ONCE the epoxy has fully dried, you can paint the outside gray part of the geode.

I love the way the gold looks with the crystals against the bright white of the dresser!

1

2

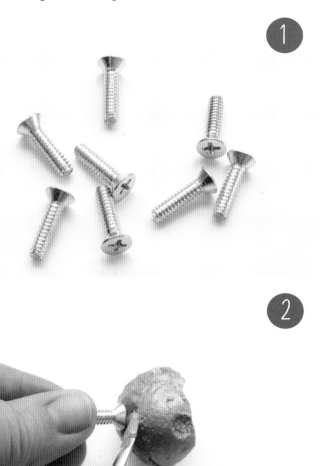

You don't have to use geodes if you don't want to. You can use plain old rocks. I think they are just as cool!

I think I am going to use these in my oldest son's new room. They are masculine and would go perfect in his already nature-inspired room.

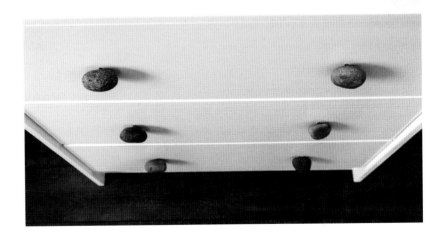

supply list:

- small rocks
- cardboard, card stock, or canvas
- pencil or printer
- epoxy
- frames

rock state art

A s I mentioned in the introduction, decorating with things from nature is a great way to remember trips and vacations. Every time we get back to the hotel room, my boys usually have a pocketful of "treasures" they have collected throughout the day. One fun way to remember your trip would be to frame some of those things you find. Maybe add them to a shadow box. The framed project I am sharing here is Rock State Art.

Collect rocks (or other small things) from the state or country you are visiting, and then create the shape of that place out of the objects you have brought home with you. We live in Utah, so I had to include that state. We also love visiting Oregon, so I made one for that state as well.

1. COLLECT the rocks, and then wash them really well. Glue will not stick well if there is any dirt on the rocks. Decide what you are going to mount the rocks on. I chose an 8 × 10 piece of canvas. I put it through my printer like paper to print the outline of the state. You can also freehand it or use a projector.

2. GLUE your rocks to the canvas or thick paper with epoxy. Start by gluing the rocks that outline the border before filling the rest of the shape in. It is easier that way, and you'll get a more defined outline.

3. ONCE you have all the rocks glued in place and it has dried completely, you can add it to the frame and hang it up to enjoy! Another fun idea would be to paint a dot in the area (or areas) of the state that you have visited. Or use a different colored rock in those areas. Hang them alone or add pictures from the trip to make a large gallery wall. No matter how you make them or display them, it will be a fun reminder of your travels there.

For another easy project, you can also glue a magnet to the back and have a decorative magnet. I used these colorful agates that I bought online to make some for our giant magnet board. I dare you to try and say agate magnet ten times. Ha!

If the next time you are outside, you start noticing rocks and wondering how you can use them, then I have succeeded. Happy hunting!

lettuce
eggs
bread
Milk
Butter
crackers

T he sea, once it casts its spell, holds one in its net of wonder forever.[1]

–Jacques-Yves Cousteau

chapter 6: beach finds

Whether you live on the beach or you only get to visit every once in awhile, you can't help but comb for treasures. Since our family doesn't get to visit very often, the few mementos we do bring home from our trip help remind us of our time there. Sometimes I add those things to a memory jar, and sometimes I make something with them.

supply list:

- glass bowl vase
- driftwood pieces
- epoxy

drift wood vase

I love working with driftwood. I knew that this weathered wood would look amazing with flowers, so I opted for a vase. I am so happy with how it turned out!

1. START by making the base. I had a round bowl vase I knew would be perfect for this project. I laid out a few pieces in a circle and then set the vase on top to see if it fit well. I made a few adjustments, and then took the vase off. I carefully added glue to each one, making sure I didn't bump them out of place. Then I set the bowl back on top of them so I could start adding the side pieces.

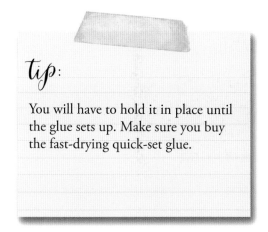

tip:

You will have to hold it in place until the glue sets up. Make sure you buy the fast-drying quick-set glue.

2. GLUE the side pieces on one by one.

3. ONCE you have the first layer of side pieces, start adding another layer on top of that.

4. DEPENDING on the size of your bowl, you may need more layers, but for me it only took two layers to reach the top. Once you reach the top, add horizontal pieces in a circle similar to the base.

The soft pink peonies were perfect for this vase!

supply list:

- shells
- drill
- small drill bit
- block of scrap wood
- fishing line
- basic pendant light
- lampshade
- superglue

shell pendant light

This is one of my favorite projects. Along with collecting rocks while growing up, I also collected shells. The whole time I was growing up I only went to the beach once, and I was too young to really remember it. I grew up here in Utah, so the beach and seashells were a thing of wonderment. Shells to me were rare and therefore as valuable as gold. Don't get me wrong, I love my mountains, but beaches hold a special place in my heart. And I have made it a point to visit as often as I can now that I am an adult and have my own family.

1. START by going through your collection of shells. If you don't have a collection, you can find them at your local craft store. Choose some that look similar to one another, and then put them in piles according to size. Take a small drill bit, and begin drilling holes in them. You will need a hole in the top of the shell and the bottom of the shell. Make sure you put a block of wood underneath so the drill has something to go into other than your work surface.

2. USE fishing line to connect the shells together because it is clear and won't be seen.

3. START stringing the shells together. I knew exactly what I wanted to use to hang mine. I bought a small IKEA lampshade. They are my favorite because you can change it from a lampshade to a ceiling pendant by twisting the center piece. Genius! As a bonus, they are inexpensive. I removed the fabric from mine.

tip:

Make sure to leave at least a few inches of fishing line at the top so you have some to tie it onto the shade later.

4. TIE the strands of shells to the top ring of the shade frame (or wherever you are hanging them). When they are all tied on, add a tiny drop of superglue to each knot to keep it from loosening from the weight of the shells over time.

When I was setting up the table over which the shells would hang, I decided I wanted to add something to the wall above the bowl of starfish. I looked around my office and saw a pile of sand dollars we had found in Oregon. I used a hot glue gun and attached them to some white card stock paper and framed them. It was super simple to do, and I love how it looks!

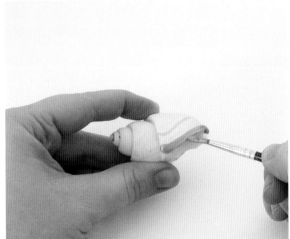

gold shells

Another super simple project is to paint shells. Originally, I was going to paint these all gold. But I just couldn't do it. I loved the patterns and textures, so I decided to paint just the edges. It still gave it a modern look without compromising the integrity of the shell's natural design.

My kids started collecting sand in bags anytime we went somewhere, even if it was just a lake. We started putting the sand in a jar and labeling it "Bear Lake" or "Cannon Beach, Oregon" depending on where we got it from. Put the sand and shells in small, decorative bottles and they can act as decor in addition to being a keepsake from a trip.

hooks

This next idea may not work if you fly to the beach, unless you have roomy luggage. If you have ever been to the beach, you know there can be a lot of driftwood. Some driftwood pieces are smoother than others, and some are much bigger than others. A larger piece looks amazing on the wall with some hooks added. It could be a place to hang swimming suits when you come in from a swim or in an entryway for your bag and set of keys when you get home from work.

Another idea for beachy hooks would be to cut individual pieces of wood out and glue a shell, starfish, or sand dollar to them.

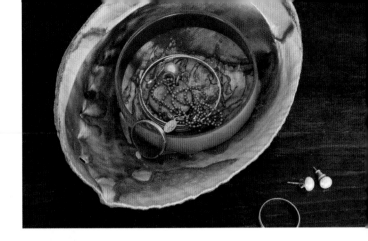

jewelry bowl

Abalone shells are beautifully iridescent on the inside. They would be a perfect place to put your jewelry on either your nightstand or makeup table. Or maybe on your entryway table for your loose change and keys.

supply list:

- hot glue gun
- starfish
- string or twine

starfish garland

This is such a simple project. And it won't take you very long either. I chose to use twine because that is what I had on hand, but you could use anything you want that would fit your decorating style.

1. USE a hot glue gun to stick the starfish to the twine. Make sure you just put a small dab so it won't show on the front side.

Then, you are ready to drape or hang it anywhere you like!

When styling the shelves to show the garland, I put some sand dollars in a tray and filled it with sand. I thought it was a fun way to show off the sand dollars.

sea glass tray

I like the whole idea of a broken and jagged piece of glass getting smoothed in the ocean after being tossed about. I love all the different colors you can find while combing the beach. I have not had the good fortune of finding a lot of it in our few trips to the beach, but I wanted to make this tray full of it. I bought some beach glass at a craft store. They didn't look like the real thing, however. They were too large and not rounded enough. So I broke them into smaller pieces and put them in my son's rock polisher for about a week. It worked perfectly! I added those pieces to the real ones I have collected over the years, and I had enough glass. I decided last minute to add some small starfish and a few small shells as well. But I love that it is mostly glass.

I made my serving tray in the same way that I built the terrarium in the plants chapter. But you can find Plexiglas trays easily at home decor stores or online. Once you have your sea glass and your Plexiglas tray, you can begin!

1. START by laying out the sea glass and other things where you want them to go in the tray.

2. MIX the two-part resin in a plastic cup according to the directions on the package.

3. I was expecting the glass to move around when the resin was poured, so I went slowly. I was happy to find they didn't move all over like I had thought. I only had to fix a couple of things that had shifted slightly. Once the resin was all poured, I blew on the tiny little bubbles that surfaced to get them to pop. The box also suggested spraying denatured alcohol onto the surface to get rid of the bubbles.

4. DRILL some holes and add handles as needed.
I just love how it turned out and that you can see through it! What a unique tray to serve drinks with next time a friend comes to visit. Plus it will remind you of your trips to the beach. This would also be a fun project to let the kids help with. They could choose what goes in the tray and help lay it out.

Whether it is simple or intricate, your ocean-themed projects can create a soothing space that will remind you of your time there.

C ome forth into the light of things, let nature be your teacher.[1]

–William Wordsworth

chapter 7: other natural elements

There are so many natural elements that you can gather and use depending on where you live. Here are some of my favorites:

ACORNS

I have a friend up the street who has a tree that drops so many of these little guys every year that she gathers buckets and buckets full of them. I have a tote full of them for whenever I need them and a bowl of them on display all of the time.

I have learned the hard way that they will mold if you do not dry them out. Whether you live in a desert and leave them out in the sun for a while or put them in your oven on a low temperature, you need to dry them.

Even though I use them year-round, I know acorns are typically associated with autumn. I use them in tablescapes in the fall.

You can string them like popcorn and make a garland. How cute would that be in a woodland-creature nursery? Scatter them down the center of the table along with your centerpiece when having guests over, glue them to a frame, or paint them. You could even add them to floral arrangements by adding wire to them.

ANTLERS

My boys love hiking. While we are in the mountains, they like to look for antlers that the yearling deer have shed. I think they look best in a vignette.

Mount it to a piece of wood and hang it on the wall for a hook or for hanging jewelry on. You could also paint them to make them a little more contemporary looking.

LEAVES

Leaves are beautiful! I love the symmetry and the many shades of green (and other colors) that they come in. Sometimes, I just add leaves in a vase for a touch of greenery.

You can press them between the pages of books and frame them. I started doing this as a kid with flowers and leaves, but I would always forget which books I put them in. My mom probably still has pressed leaves in her many books in her office!

When you think of bringing leaves in, you probably think of colorful fall foliage. In my opinion, that is the best time to gather leaves. I wish fall lasted longer here in Utah. I frame them as well as put them in vases.

PUMPKINS

While we are on the subject of fall, pumpkins are another favorite of mine. You can leave them as they are, paint them, or add a little metallic detail by using brads.

My favorite pumpkins are the white ones. When I grow pumpkins in my garden, I make sure to plant some of these.

I like them for many reasons, but the main reason is they don't look as "fall-ish" as the orange ones, so I can incorporate them into my everyday decor and not just my holiday decorating.

HERBS, FRUITS, AND VEGGIES

If you don't cook using fresh herbs, try it! It is a game changer! Amazing. I plant them in my garden every year, but in the winter, I have several pots in my kitchen. They either make their home on my open shelving or next to the sink.

You probably have a fruit bowl. But you probably didn't really think of it as a decoration. I love to add fruit and veggies to centerpieces, in decorative bowls on the table for every day, and on the kitchen shelves. They can look good while they waiting to be eaten, especially if they have come fresh from the garden. Why not show them off a bit?

FEATHERS

This one makes my boys happy. They love feathers. I do clean them well if they are feathers the kids have collected. I clean just about everything that comes from outside before I use it inside. Since different birds molt at different times of the year, you are sure to find all sorts of feathers, no matter the season. You can also buy them from craft stores if you need more variety.

Really the only two ways I use them is in a vase or frame. Both are great ways to display them. They pair well with fall decor as well. My son made a garland for his room and added feathers. It was quite beautiful, although I am sure he was going for "cool." I have seen people paint feather edges gold. You could also add them to a flower arrangement. I think I am going to add some to my potted plants now that the book is done and I have all these feathers that need homes. However you use them, they bring a texture to a space like nothing else can.

PINECONES

These have an amazing texture and feel! They are pretty easy to come by too. I use them all time.

supply list:

- pinecones
- branch clippers
- hot glue gun
- mirror

pinecone mirror

Staining this mirror was one of the first "projects" I did as a married person. I bought the mirror unfinished and stained it myself. I have had it for almost fifteen years and decided it needed a new look. We have a giant pine tree in our backyard that gives us a plethora of pinecones. We have more pinecones than we know what to do with!

1. CUT the pinecones in half so you have a flat side to work with.

2. USE a hot glue gun to attach the pinecones to the mirror. I tried to do even rows, but there were a few places I had to add a small pinecone in to fill a void.

3. TRY propping it up on your shelves instead of hanging it as you traditionally do with mirrors.

I use pinecones in vignettes, in tablescapes, and in bowls (of course!) around the house. I tuck them just about anywhere. Most of the time, I leave them as is, but I did paint some gold for the tablescape you will see on page 160. I also painted some with a thick layer of white so they would look porcelain.

supply list:

- metal tray
- pea-sized gravel (rinsed)
- potting soil
- Irish moss

I live in the desert, so moss is not found as easily as in more humid climates, but we do have some growing on the north side of the garage and on the north side of the garage's roof (it is the original wood-shingle roof from the 1930s). When it falls, I stick it in my terrariums and dream of living somewhere lush and green. And when I go on walks in the mountains and see some in the shade of a large tree, I take a picture. But there is one kind of moss I can plant and have success with. Even though it is meant for outdoors, I plant it temporarily inside to enjoy.

moss in metal tray

The type of moss I used for this project is Irish moss that is traditionally used in rock gardens and in between pavers for walkways. I have some in the walkway in my secret garden, and I needed to plant some more due to some getting shaded by other plants and dying off. But before I planted it outside, I decided to enjoy it inside for a bit. Like I mentioned before, not everything in decorating needs to be permanent. Just like a flower arrangement will eventually die and need to be thrown away, some living things eventually grow too large to be easily accommodated inside. Sometimes, they only thrive long-term if they are outdoors. I kept the moss in the tray for about a month before transplanting it outside.

1. START with a simple metal tray. I actually made this tray in metal shop in junior high. I decided it was the perfect "planter" for the moss. I added gravel to the bottom since it doesn't have drainage holes.

2. ADD the soil.

3. ADD the moss plants to the tray.

For this girl who loves moss but lives in a desert, this was fun to have hanging out for a bit on my bookshelf.

moss initials on stump

I added some dried moss to a tree stump with hot glue for a Valentine's Day mantel, but I think it would look cute displayed year-round on a shelf or bookcase.

I hope your walks on the beach, in the mountains, around the park, or wherever you live take on new meaning. I hope you find things and give them a new life. Even if it is just temporary, you can use them to make your home more interesting and more beautiful.

Land really is the best art.[1]

–Andy Warhol

chapter 8: displaying photos of nature

I grew up with sisters who didn't love getting dirty like I did. So in the back of my mind while writing this book, I could hear a voice saying things like, "I don't want to bring anything dirty inside." I get it. Believe it or not, I am a bit of a germaphobe. So let's say that every single project in this book is not something you would do, then *this* chapter is for you! And even if you are a gathering fool like me, there are still some things you can't gather. There are some amazing things in nature that you simply can't bring home. That is when taking photographs comes in handy. And you do not need a fancy camera. Some of these pictures I took with my (outdated) cell phone.

So let's chat about different ways to display the photos you take of nature.

PROP IT UP!

I love to use my photos as enlargements. It depends on where you print them, but I can print a 16 × 20 for around twelve dollars and a 20 × 30 for less than twenty dollars. That's pretty inexpensive art! And it will have more meaning to you than something you bought. You can hang it on the wall, or you can prop it up. It can even function as a way to hide an electrical outlet or something else that you may not want to be the focal point. My favorite way to prop up art is on a shelf.

If your photograph is in a location where it needs to be protected, such as in the kitchen, add a thin layer of Plexiglas in front of the picture.

A DIFFERENT WAY TO HANG THEM

There is nothing wrong with hanging art from a nail in the wall. Most of mine is hung that way. But maybe shake it up a bit, and try a different way. String some wire across the wall and hang the photos with clips. I got this set from IKEA. It makes an interesting wall feature, and it is easily changed out.

Wire or String

If you don't want to use wire, you could use ribbon, rope, twine, or string. You can make it fit your own personal style.

Hanging from a Branch

This idea could be really dramatic if you have really high ceilings and you use a large branch. I like the idea of hanging it above a sofa as well. I think it is fun to be creative when displaying photos, especially ones that are artistic. You can hang the branch like the one on page 145, or put it in a large floor vase and hang the photos like ornaments.

DITCH THE FRAME

Picture Holders

Who says you need to frame a picture? Why not find other ways to display them? I used my rock candlesticks with a little wire added to display some photos of the beach. The smooth stones seemed to fit in perfectly with the beachy pictures.

tip:

Use spray adhesive to glue card stock, chipboard, or cardboard to the back of the photo so it will be stiffer and hang straight.

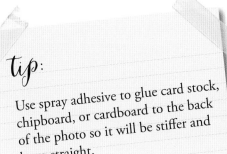

picture blocks

I made a version of this about eight or nine years ago and hung it in my hallway, so when I was thinking of ways you can display photographs of nature, I knew I wanted to share how I had created mine. It is a fairly simple project and looks great with just a small gathering of photos, as shown here, or would be amazing as a full wall gallery!

1. CUT out the pieces from plywood using a table saw. I had 5 × 7 pieces and 8 × 10 pieces. They were mostly cut from ½-inch plywood, but a couple I cut out of ⅛-inch plywood so I had even more variety. Sand them a little, being careful not to round the edges. Use a sanding block to ensure the edges stay crisp.

2. YOU can leave some alone, or you can glue them together in varying thicknesses. For example, some might have two, three, or four layers. Glue and then clamp them while they dry. You could also use a brad nailer with finishing nails to nail each layer on.

3. BARE wood needs to be sealed, so brush on a couple of layers of polyurethane.

4. ONCE the polyurethane dries, you can use spray adhesive to attach your photos to the blocks. I sprayed both the back of the photo and the block.

PHOTO SPLIT UP

If you have access to some sort of photo editing software (there are free ones online to chose from), then you can use a grid to help divide a photo into sections and crop it. I cropped my photo into a square before splitting it up. You could take a landscape shot and split it up into three sections. You could make it into a ton of smaller pieces too. Turn the photo into a puzzle! Or maybe into a shape like a heart. There really is no limit to what you can do.

I encourage you to take a camera with you wherever you go. You never know when you will see something that would make amazing art for your home.

One touch of nature makes the whole world kin.[1]

–William Shakespeare

chapter 9: styling tablescapes and vignettes

My house is small, and any entertaining we do has to happen in the warmer months when we can host outside in our yard, and even then, we are super casual about it. Think barbeque and paper plates. Until a few years ago, I had never done a full tablescape. The most I had ever done was a flower arrangement or some candles. I was challenged by a company to do a tablescape one fall, and I have been hooked ever since. Most of the time I still keep it very simple, but I do like to add more things every now and then. My house hasn't magically gotten bigger, so I still can't host large dinner parties, but I do find excuses to decorate for just my family. This book also gave me an excuse to play around with different styles. I had fun!

In the following chapter, I give some examples of very simple tables and some that are a bit more layered. The point I hope to make is that you can use what you have, and it doesn't have to be perfect or elaborate. Your guests will appreciate anything that you do beyond the norm.

pink and gold

I am not an overly pink kind of person. I can usually only handle a little here and there. So I was surprised that I loved this table so much. I think it is the gold teapot. Everyone should have a gold teapot! I love using items as vases that are not actually vases. The black, pink, white, gold, and green color scheme has become a favorite of mine.

eggs (yes, eggs!)

When I was thinking about what to use for a "springtime" table, eggs came to mind. Maybe it is because we have chickens, but I thought it was a fun example of something you could use. I added vinyl initials to the eggs, but you could use a marker or paint as well. Springtime flowers and sky-blue plates tie it all together! I used an old fence post as the table runner. Don't worry, I scrubbed and scrubbed it before using it. The eggs were sanitized as well. Deep breaths, fellow germaphobes! Deep breaths!

tip:

Hard boil the eggs before decorating with them.

summer casual

D o you need a simple idea you can throw together last minute? Cut some flowers from your yard, or grab some at the store. Put them in all the little glass jars, vases, bottles, and containers that you have all over your house. Line them up or add them to a tray for a centerpiece.

beachy

S ummer makes me think of lots of things, including the beach. Simply add shells, starfish, or coral to a table with beachy colors, and you are set. If you have a larger table than mine, some white flowers would be a nice touch as well. Maybe add some small shells to the bottom of the clear vase the flowers are in, or add a layer of sand inside the vase.

flowerpot as a place card

Do you like to give your guests a little party favor? Why not a small potted plant? Share the love of nature with them! The little gift can also act as a place card. I added some vinyl lettering to mine, but you could use paint as well or paint your pot with chalkboard paint and write guests' names with chalk.

green and gold

I know what some of you are thinking. I hear that little voice in my head again. Some of you are panicking that there is dirt on the table . . . on the *plate* no less. It's okay. You can skip this one if you want. The rest of us will use them as place holders and gifts for the guests. And aren't the plates they are on amazing? For those of you opposed to a potted plant, some leaves gathered together with ribbon or string on the napkin would create a similar effect.

fruits and vegetables

Why not go shopping in your garden or refrigerator for table decorations? Fruits and veggies are gorgeous! There are so many colors to choose from too. You can do an all-green theme, or you can add as many colors as you want. I use lemons a lot, so I almost always have some on hand. Lemons are not just for the water. Add them as your centerpiece and place card holders!

stick table runner

Remember the chapter on branches, sticks, and stumps? We've put the stick table runner (see page 101) to use in this tablescape. It adds so much texture to the table! And it doesn't have to be a fall tablescape. The stick runner will look terrific in any season.

pumpkin vase

Pumpkins, gourds, or even eggplants can be hollowed out and used as a vase for the night. Don't have any flowers? Cut some branches or add some leaves.

leaves

One time, I had to come up with a fall tablescape at the last minute. Because my table is small, it can be a challenge to decorate. I decided to gather some leaves and just scatter them down the center. I came inside from gathering leaves in my yard and noticed that they happened to be stacked according to color because of the order I collected them in. It looked like a rainbow! So instead of just randomly scattering them, I placed them in order and added my favorite candlesticks.

winter

Just because you are hosting during the holidays doesn't mean you have to have a traditional holiday decor on your table. Go with more of a winter theme. Pinecones and small trees work well.

Add as much or as little as you want, but please don't stress! Use what you have already paired with things from nature and you can come up with some beautiful tablescapes that will make you want to entertain more often.

odd numbers

Confession . . . I am not a big vignette person. I like to style a side table here and there and the fireplace mantel and shelves in my office. But it has never been super practical to have pretty things on all the surfaces, especially the low—very reachable—ones, when you're living with four children. And by now you should know I like to keep things simple. When I look through magazine and blogs, I love when people layer and layer, but when I try to do that in my own home it just doesn't feel like me. So here is my take on vignettes: Do what feels right to you. If it makes you twitchy to have too many things on your counters and other surfaces, then simplify and only have a few important things. If you love to display a lot of things at a time and have a very collected and layered look, do it! The best thing about decorating is that the right way is your way. It is your home. You should do things the way you like and not the way a magazine or celebrity tells you it should be done. Do what fits your space and your lifestyle.

No matter how many items you chose to add, there are a few key points to keep in mind:

Place things in odd numbers. Three is a good number for me. A stack of books, a vase of flowers, a rock. Boom. It can be that simple. Or if you have a larger area, use several small groups of threes, fives, and so on. This is not a hard-and-fast rule though. It's just something to help you when you are styling.

varying heights

Sometimes, I like to have something (a mantel, for instance) that includes accessory decor of all the same height. For example, I'll line up five identical vases in a row filled with branches with leaves or flowers. It can make an impact. But most of the time, I like to have things all different heights. If what you want to use needs a little extra height, add some books or possibly a tree stump under it.

diagonal lines

As with other guidelines I'm offering, this one is just a suggestion based on what tends to look best. You don't have to do it every single time, but it helps to keep it in mind. Whenever I am styling something (especially shelves), I try to think about making diagonal lines. I try not to line up all of the blue things or all of the plants. Here are some examples:

BLACK AND WHITE SHELVES

I have done the diagonal trick for so long that I don't always focus on it, and I put things where I think they look best and then realize afterward how many diagonal lines there are. That was the case with these shelves.

This is not a bookshelf, but I almost always include books in my vignettes. Often they are decorating books. All of the other books (such as novels) are in bookcases. If you have only a few piles of books, it looks best if they are not lined up straight but rather offset diagonally from one another. I've added dark lines to this image to help you understand the concept.

Since this setup is all white and black, I had to be mindful to not have all the black on one side and all the white on the other. I just tried to spread them out, and it ended up making diagonal lines. It really is quite easy to do once you become aware that in trying to make things look "balanced," your brain is actually looking for patterns.

As with the black items, I spread out the white objects diagonally. You may also notice that there are three black things, three white things, and three green things in this vignette. So even though they are not grouped together, I still had odd numbers of things.

COFFEE TABLE

There wasn't a lot of space to work with, but I made sure the plants were on opposite sides and the colorful books didn't line up.

OFFICE SHELVES

These shelves are in my office, and I restyle them often. The other day I was feeling like I needed more yellow in my life, so I added a few yellow things and some flowers.

These shelves act mostly as storage for all the little things I use, such as photographs, office supplies, and so on, so I have a lot of baskets and boxes.

BOOK SHELF

This is a new bookshelf I recently bought, and while it will not stay like this when I put it in it a new spot, I had fun decorating it with items from nature for this shoot.

Once again, I have the books spread out. You don't have to have them perfectly diagonal like this. Maybe you'll choose to have some line up and some not. I always have baskets and boxes and bins on shelves. Our house is small, and I add storage wherever I can. I don't think I could style a shelf of any kind without adding at least one plant. The more the merrier! Make sure to use those diagonal lines in the placement of the plants too.

VARYING TEXTURES

When styling anything, think about the different textures you are using. Some things are shiny, while others have a dull, rough look. Some have a pattern while some do not. Some items are hard while others are soft. I try to have a plant or flower, something metallic or glass, and then some other type of element like books, baskets, bowls, or tree stumps.

I bought myself this vintage brass frog because I collected frogs growing up (real and figurines). This geometric terrarium is one of my favorite possessions.

While I am not huge into having vignettes everywhere (we discussed why earlier), I do like the idea of a tray. You can style it, and then when you need the surface of you coffee table to be more functional, you simply move the tray.

I love having rough things paired with soft things. These tulips next to the tree stump make me happy. Then of course there is the shiny gold vase they are in.

When you are going for rustic, beachy, or earthy, you need to add a touch of bling or shine to break up the other textures. That is why I chose a silver frame and vase instead of going with white for both.

If you have not styled vignettes because you were too intimidated to try, I promise it is simple once you get started. Keep these guidelines in mind as you are choosing items. Just play around with them, and have fun. No design police are going to show up and tell you did it wrong. Your mother-in-law may be another matter.

Think about functionality and what is best for your home. Add natural elements and things that have personal meaning, and you can't go wrong!

I could not ask
for more

conclusion

I hope you have enjoyed reading this book as much as I have enjoyed pulling together all the projects. If you come away with a desire to add more natural elements into your home, whether it be through doing some of these projects or just displaying your finds, I will feel like I have succeeded. I truly do believe all homes and people benefit from having natural elements, especially plants. Good luck on your journey to creating a beautiful and functional space!

text sources

CHAPTER 1

1. E. E. Cummings, *Xaipe* (Oxford: Oxford University Press, 1950).

CHAPTER 2

1. Aristotle, *On Parts of Animals*, book 1, 645.a16.

CHAPTER 3

1. Hans Christian Andersen, "The Butterfly," 1861, last modified December 13, 2007, http://hca.gilead.org.il/butterfl.html.

CHAPTER 4

1. John Burroughs, *The Gospel of Nature* (Carlisle, MA: Applewood Books, 1989).

CHAPTER 6

1. Jacques Ives-Cousteau, quoted in Vikas Khatri's *Greatest Wonders of the World* (New Delhi: V&S, 2012).

CHAPTER 7

1. William Wordsworth, "The Tables Turned," Poetry Foundation, http://www.poetry-foundation.org/poem/174826.

CHAPTER 8

1. Andy Warhol, in Charles Moffat "Andy Warhol, Pop Artist: The Prince of Pop Art," The Art History Archive, last modified November 2007, http://www.arthistoryarchive.com/arthistory/popart/Andy-Warhol.html.

CHAPTER 9

1. William Shakespeare, *Troilus and Cressida*, 3.3, http://shakespeare.mit.edu/troilus_cressida/troilus_cressida.3.3.html.

material sources

BIRCH LANE

- Metal chairs (page 177), http://www.birchlane.com/Birch-Lane-Harmon-Dining-Chair-BL3723.html.

BLOG PROJECTS (*NOT JUST A HOUSEWIFE*)

- Barnwood shelves in office (page 175), http://www.notjustahousewife.net/2011/12/reclaimed-wood-floating-shelves.html.

- Bedside table—navy (page 73), http://www.notjustahousewife.net/2014/10/card-catalog-side-table.html.

- Entryway table (page 123), http://www.notjustahousewife.net/2014/10/how-to-build-a-simple-entryway-table.html.

- Gold side table (page 171), http://www.notjustahousewife.net/2014/04/gold-table-makeover.html.

- Silver circle lamp (page 99), http://www.notjustahousewife.net/2011/03/another-scrap-wood-lamp.html.

- Wood tray (page 50), http://www.notjustahousewife.net/2013/07/how-to-build-wood-serving-tray.html.

DECOART

- 3D glass paint (pages 63 and 66), http://decoart.com/glasspaint/gloss-enamels.

EBAY & ETSY

- Hairpin legs (pages 16 and 88).

HOME GOODS

- Gold teapot (page 152).
- Silver vase (page 188).
- Tall turquoise vase (page 130).

HOUZZ

- Floating shelf bracket (page 86), http://www.houzz.com/photos/10877246/Punky-Hill-Invisible-Shelf-Brackets-for-Floating-Shelf-Appearance-8-contemporary-storage-and-organization.

IKEA

- Botanical print with flowers (page 13).
- Cream fabric-covered storage boxes (page 176), http://www.ikea.com/us/en/catalog/products/30256669/#/90256690.
- Dark turquoise plates (page 154).
- Gray baskets (page 138), http://www.ikea.com/us/en/catalog/products/00159014/.
- Lighter turquoise plates (page 153).
- Shelf brackets (page 100), http://www.ikea.com/us/en/catalog/products/10136135/#/90136136.
- Silver lamp (page 117), http://www.ikea.com/us/en/catalog/products/70089584/.
- Wire hanging system (page 144), http://www.ikea.com/us/en/catalog/products/60075295/.
- Yellow armchair (page 17), http://www.ikea.com/us/en/catalog/products/50262872/#/70262890.

- Yellow striped bowl (page 21), http://www.ikea.com/us/en/catalog/products/90234863/.
- White coffee table (pages 171 and 173), http://www.ikea.com/us/en/catalog/products/90208449/#/50208451.

LAMPS PLUS

- Brass lamp (page 111), http://www.lampsplus.com/products/Robert-Abbey-Kinetic-Antique-Brass-Pharmacy-Desk-Lamp__86934.html.

MICHAELS

- Cork frame mats (page 176).
- Gold spray paint (pages 34 and 83), Design Master, http://www.michaels.com/design-master-premium-metals-spray-24kt-pure-gold/10211540.html.
- Metal letter *r* (page 176), http://www.michaels.com/studio-decor-galvanized-letter-r-7-in/10352725.html#q=metal+letter&start=7.

MY BARNWOOD FRAMES

- Reclaimed wood barnwood farm table (pages 151, 157, 159, 163), http://mybarnwoodframes.com/barnwood-and-reclaimed-wood-furniture/barnwood-tables.

PROFLOWERS

- Polygon terrarium (page 179), Red Envelope, http://products.proflowers.com/gifts/polygon-glass-terrarium-30116123.

SOCIETY6

- Bohemian throw pillow (page 24), http://society6.com/product/bohemian-zoy_pillow#25=193&18=126.
- Deer print (page 93), Craftberry, http://society6.com/product/buck-watercolor_print#1=45.

TARGET

- Black-and-white baskets (page 12), Nate Berkus Collection.
- Black, white, and gold plates (page 152), Nate Berkus Collection.
- Gold basket with plant in it (page 84), Nate Berkus Collection.
- Round gold box (page 111), Nate Berkus Collection.
- Small cream geometric vase (page 87), Nate Berkus Collection.
- White bowls with dots (page 158).
- Wood bowl (pages 138 and 123).

THE GRAPHICS FAIRY

- Botanical fern prints (page 178), http://thegraphicsfairy.com/?s=ferns.

URBAN OUTFITTERS

- White faceted vase (page 173).

WALMART

- Bookcase (page 176): Better Homes and Gardens Collection, http://www.walmart.com/ip/Better-Homes-and-Gardens-Crossmill-Collection-5-Shelf-Bookcase-Lintel-Oak/35910937.
- Lampshade (page 98), Better Homes and Gardens Collection, http://www.walmart.com/ip/Better-Homes-and-Gardens-BH43-020-499-35-Better-Homes-and-Gardens-Linen-Drum-Shade/28860080.
- Metal basket (page 93), Better Homes and Gardens Collection, http://www.walmart.com/ip/Better-Homes-and-Gardens-Medium-Wire-Basket-with-Chalkboard-Black/24534322.
- Round metal bin (page 108), Better Homes and Gardens Collection, http://www.walmart.com/ip/Better-Homes-and-Gardens-Galvanized-Round-Bin-Silver/24534332.
- Square plates and bowls (page 164), Better Homes and Garden Collection, http://www.walmart.com/ip/Better-Homes-and-Gardens-Porcelain-Square-16-piece-Dinnerware-Set/24076922.
- White scalloped plates (page 164), Better Homes and Gardens Collection, http://www.walmart.com/ip/Better-Homes-and-Gardens-10.5-Scalloped-Dinner-Plates-White-Set-of-6/37897143.

WAYFAIR

- Lenox French Perle plates (page 158), http://www.wayfair.com/Lenox-French-Perle-11-Dinner-Plate-LNX5125.html?piid%5B0%5D=9907363.

Places I buy my terrarium plants:

- Josh's Frogs (Plants for terrariums and vivariums), http://www.joshsfrogs.com/live-plants/houseplants.html.

- Hirt's Gardens on Amazon, http://www.amazon.com/gp/product/B009CBIFGO/ref=oh_aui_detailpage_o06_s00?ie=UTF8&psc=1.

- I buy larger ferns at both Home Depot and Olson's Garden Shoppe

For more information on bonding Plexiglas, I recommend watching the video series "How to build an aquarium 1–6."

- King of DIY, https://www.youtube.com/watch?v=3rsUbzVwaUo

index

about the author

Stacy Risenmay grew up in a small town in Utah where she spent most of her time outdoors and rarely wore shoes. After living several other places, she has returned to live in Utah with her family. Stacy and her husband of fifteen years have four boys, which suits her tomboy personality just fine. She is the author of the popular home decor blog *Not Just a Housewife*, where she shares the adventures of fixing up their 1938 cottage-style home.